JESUS THE KING
IS COMING

JESUS THE KING IS COMING

CHARLES LEE FEINBERG
Editor

MOODY PRESS
CHICAGO

ISBN: 0-8024-4331-1

Library of Congress Catalog Card Number: 74-15351

Printed in the United States of America

Contents

5

CONTRIBUTORS

S. MAXWELL CODER, D. D.
Dean Emeritus, Moody Bible Institute, Chicago, Illinois

CHARLES LEE FEINBERG, TH.D., PH.D.
Dean, Professor of Semitics and Old Testament, Talbot Theological Seminary, La Mirada, California

DANIEL FUCHS, D.D.
Executive Secretary, American Board of Missions to the Jews, Inc., Englewood Cliffs, New Jersey

WENDELL G. JOHNSTON, TH.D.
President, Detroit Bible College, Detroit, Michigan

HAL LINDSAY, TH.M.
Author, Lecturer, Los Angeles, California

CLARENCE E. MASON, JR. D.D.
Scofield Professor of Bible Exposition, Philadelphia College of Bible, Philadelphia, Pennsylvania

JOHN F. WALVOORD, D.D., TH.D.
President, Dallas Theological Seminary, Dallas, Texas

7

Foreword

THE SEVENTH CONGRESS on Prophecy was convened in the greater New York area under the guidance of the Holy Spirit by the American Board of Missions to the Jews. Its theme was most timely in view of world events: Jesus is Coming—for His Church, to Israel, and to the nations. As we observe the alignment of nations, the Common Market, Russia and China growing in strength and their striving for control of the Mid-East through the Arab states, we cannot fail to recognize that prophetic Scriptures are being fulfilled in our day. This is especially true when we see Israel, alone and surrounded by enemies, a pawn in world power politics, back in her land as a living, modern nation and celebrating her 25th anniversary.

As it was during the 1967 congress, so it was in 1973: the world was on the threshhold of another outbreak of war in that strategic area of the world. Surely, the night draws to a close; the Day Star will soon arise (2 Pe 1:19).

The times called for a reaffirmation of the blessed hope of believers and the events that will follow that wondrous happening. This challenge called for men able to "rightly divide the word of truth." So invitations went to a select group of Bible scholars, able teachers of the prophetic Word. These men were assigned the task of presenting a clear reaffirmation of the great prophetic themes of God's Word as they relate to our Lord Jesus Christ, the Church, the nations, and Israel. The task was well accomplished, as attested to by the blessings which came to all who attended the congress. This book, which presents the major messages of the congress, continues the inspiration and illumination of that week.

To encourage all to witness, there was a missionary presentation each evening in which faithful missionaries shared the joys of victories won as the good news of God's love has been proclaimed to Jew and Gentile.

We recognize with gratitude the three churches which hosted the congress; Calvary Baptist Church of New York City; Franklin Avenue Baptist Church of Malvern, New York; and Long Hill Chapel of Chatham, New Jersey. The churches and their fine staffs truly made us welcome.

We are grateful to the speakers of the congress for permitting us to publish these messages and for finding time in their busy schedules to prepare the manuscripts, and especially to our dear friend Dr. Charles Lee Feinberg for undertaking the responsibilities of editorship in spite of a heavy work load.

Above all, our grateful praise goes to our heavenly Father who permitted us to gather in such a Congress on Prophecy and to enlarge the outreach and blessings of that ministry through this book.

May the soon-coming of our precious Lord become more wonderful and real to all who read this book. With John we cry, "Even so, come, Lord Jesus" (Rev 22:20).

EMIL D. GRUEN
Conference Director

Preface

IT IS WITHOUT PRECEDENT. Over three decades, a series of national congresses on Israel and prophecy have been conducted in this country. During the tragic days of World War II the first conference met in Calvary Baptist Church, in New York City, November 1-8, 1942. The post-war years served only to bring into clearer focus the broad outlines of prophetic truth emphasized then by able expositors. Along with such giants in the Scriptures as Lewis Sperry Chafer, Leopold Cohn, and Harry Ironside, twenty-three others participated in that historic event.

During the intervening years, and the epoch-making events of the War of Independence with the founding of the State of Israel (1948), and the conflicts of 1956 and 1967, congresses met periodically. The *Sixth Congress on Prophecy,* convened in New York in 1970, marked the Diamond Jubilee of the American Board of Missions to the Jews, founded in 1894 by Dr. Leopold Cohn. The concluding congress in the series met in May, 1973, again in Calvary Baptist Church of New York City.

Any reader who takes the time to compare these congress addresses, now in printed form, will readily discern the same fidelity to the infallibility and inerrancy of the whole Word of God; the same approach to Bible interpretation by way of the premillennial, dispensational position; and the same genuine longing for the appearing of the Lord Jesus Christ for His bride and the consummation of God's entire prophetic program.

11

The messages cover the broad areas of prophecy: Christ, the Church, Israel, and the Gentiles. They have been arranged in a somewhat chronological order—the last days of the Church age, the rapture, the Tribulation, the judgment of the nations, the resurrections, and the Millennium. Because the subjects of the addresses did not fit in every instance the successive events of the future, but were broader in scope, a strict chronological arrangement was not feasible. This should in no wise impair the effectiveness and force of any of the messages.

Contributors to this volume are able expositors of the Scriptures, and leaders well-reported by the brethren. The editor extends warm thanks for their cooperation. To Dr. Emil D. Gruen, gracious conference host, and to all host pastors of cooperating churches, our thanks. Finally, our gratitude is expressed to God for the manifold blessings of the conference— and in a special sense for His goodness in permitting Dr. John F. Walvoord, president of Dallas Theological Seminary, seminary classmate, colleague, and friend, and the editor himself, to participate in the entire series of congresses.

May God alone receive glory as His children experience the blessings of this volume. May unsaved Jews and Gentiles who read these messages learn to trust Christ as Saviour.

CHARLES LEE FEINBERG

1

The Last Days of the Church on Earth

JOHN F. WALVOORD

ONE OF THE PENETRATING QUESTIONS to be faced in our modern day is whether we are in the last days of the Church on Earth. It is answered in the Word of God and in contemporary events. Prophecy in the Bible sometimes deals with the nations, or the Gentiles. Many chapters in the Old Testament, as well as in the New, deal with the subject of the nations in God's prophetic program.

Another great subject is that of Israel in prophecy, beginning with the revelation to Abraham concerning his seed and the promised land. This line of truth can be traced through the Scriptures.

One of the lines of prophecy especially dear to the hearts of the saints today is the truth as it relates to the Church, "our truth" as it were, truth concerning our present and our future. The prophecies that relate to the Church fall into two major classifications:

First, there is prophecy that relates to the Church as the body of Christ. Here the great truth predicted in the Bible is revealed that in this present age God will call out from Jew and Gentile alike a people to His name—those who will put their trust in Christ, be placed into the body of Christ by the baptism of His

Spirit, and enter into God's glorious program of making the Church, His body, the supreme demonstration of His grace. The future of the Church unfolds in many New Testament passages which reveal the Lord's coming for His Church.

Christ promised that, having gone to heaven to prepare a place for us, He would "come again to receive us unto Himself, that where He is there we may be also" (Jn 14:1-3). Believers can anticipate with joy the blessed hope that one day Christ is coming, that the dead in Christ will be raised, and living Christians will be caught up to meet Him in the air. The prophetic Word reveals that we will proceed to heaven to join Christ in the symbol of marriage, be judged at the judgment seat of Christ, and be rewarded for what we have done for the Lord. This is just the beginning of an eternity with the Lord.

In addition to these blessed truths that relate to the Church as the body of Christ, prophecies relate to the professing church, to Christendom. This body of truth is quite different than the body of truth that relates to the true Church. The Scriptures which speak of the organized church in the last days predict that the professing church will depart from the faith and become increasingly apostate as the age climaxes.

Apostasy, or departure from the faith, is not a peculiarity of the organized church. It began, of course, in the Garden of Eden when Satan raised the question of doubt, "Hath God said?" Throughout the Old Testament the people of Israel were sometimes in periods of revival and blessing, and sometimes in periods of apostasy and judgment. In the New Testament, the same tendency toward apostasy that led Israel astray from the Word of God and His plan for them, is found in the professing church ever since the first century. It is very significant that the Bible anticipates this.

One of the broad prophecies of apostasy is given in 1 Timothy where the prediction is:

> Now the Spirit speaketh expressly that in the latter times some shall depart from the faith, giving heed to seducing spirits,

and doctrines of devils, speaking lies in hypocrisy, having their conscience seared with a hot iron, forbidding to marry, and commanding to abstain from meats, which God hath created to be received with thanksgiving of them which believe and know the truth (1 Ti 5:1-3).

The apostle Paul predicted that as the church moved on to its consummation, the true Church, the body of Christ, would be caught up to be with the Lord, while the professing church would increasingly depart from the faith.

Tracing apostasy as it relates to the Church through history, one finds some significant facts. First, in the early centuries of the Church, the first major defection was a denial of the premillennial return of Jesus Christ. Greek philosophy began to penetrate the Alexandrian school of theology, which foolishly attempted to combine Christian truth with Platonic philosophy. As a result, they minimized the precious truth of the second coming of Christ to bring in His millennial Kingdom.

This was followed by a second major apostasy, this one in the doctrine of grace. The great theologian, Augustine—who to some extent rescued the church from the more extreme departures of the Alexandrian school of theology—furthered the concept that grace was expressed or mediated through the church and its sacraments; that only through this means could a person enter into the grace of God. This, of course, obscured the great doctrine of justification by faith.

The Protestant reformers built upon Augustine, but they attempted to recover this great doctrine of grace. To some extent they did reaffirm the great doctrine of justification by faith. But the great truths recovered by the reformers were in due time erased by further departure from the faith, as unbelief, rationalism, and false mysticism overtook the church. Many departed from the true doctrine of the Scriptures as the authoritative, inerrant, and inspired Word of God. What is now called liberalism or modernism began to invade the Protestant church as a whole.

In our twentieth century, this first step in denial of the Bible as the true Word of God has continued until there has been an attack upon Jesus Christ, the incarnate Word of God. Today, within the church, there are denials of His deity, His virgin birth, His eternity, and other distinctive doctrines set forth in the Scriptures as to the person and work of Christ. Writers in our generation have been quite free, not only to deny the virgin birth, but also to deny that Jesus Christ actually died upon the cross for our sins, that He rose bodily from the dead, and that He is coming again.

More recently there has appeared within the church a doctrine that is almost unbelievable, the so-called teaching that God is dead. Theologians *within the church* deny the central concept that God exists, and affirm that the historic revelation of God in the Scriptures is a myth. This is what Paul was talking about when he said to Timothy, "Now the Spirit speaketh expressly that in the latter times some shall depart from the faith" (1 Ti 4:1). We do not need to wait to see this prophecy fulfilled. This prophecy is already being fulfilled.

This text anticipates precisely what is occurring today—those who depart from the faith will give heed to seducing spirits and doctrines of devils or demons. One of the outstanding features of modern religion is that there has not only been departure from biblical Christianity, but also there has been an increasing tendency to turn to demonism and the occult as a source of religious information. While this has always characterized the so-called heathen world, it has penetrated our society to an amazing extent. Reports of attention to demonism and satanic influence in our modern day appear amazingly under the guise of religion, to such an extent that so-called churches today actually worship Satan instead of the true God.

The prophecy in 1 Timothy 4 states that these false teachers will speak lies in hypocrisy. It will not come as a sincere religious effort, but rather will be a deliberate attempt to foist upon the world that which they themselves know to be a lie. The

Scriptures here rightly describe them as having consciences seared with a hot iron, insensitive to any moral principles.

Other departures from truth that exist in the name of religion will be evident, such as forbidding to marry. A large section of the church still will not permit its priests to marry, and until recently has forbidden foods which God created to be received with thanksgiving by those who know the truth. Through the centuries there have been cults with strange teachings in regard to the food they eat. These have penetrated some of the occult groups that exist. This Scripture verse, written so long ago, is not some strange anticipation of the future—it has been fulfilled all too literally in our day.

The apostle Peter, as he faced martyrdom, devoted two out of three chapters of his final epistle to describe apostasy. According to 2 Peter 2-3, apostasy will develop along three lines: First, apostasy will develop along the line of a denial of the person and work of Christ. The prophecy is recorded, "But there were false prophets also among the people, even as there shall be false teachers among you, who privily shall bring in damnable heresies, even denying the Lord that bought them and bring upon themselves swift destruction" (2 Pe 2:1). In other words, the false teachers will be characterized as those who attack the true person and work of Christ.

Like the prophecy of 1 Timothy, this prophecy does not await fulfillment; it has already been fulfilled. Today, there are those who masquerade as religious leaders who deny the person of Christ, His true deity and humanity, and His work on the cross, that He actually died as our Lamb, as our substitute and propitiation for sin.

In 2 Peter 2, most of the chapter deals with moral apostasy. It reveals the hypocrisy and emptiness that characterize those who have departed from a true doctrine of the person and work of Christ. This, too, characterizes the day in which we live. People who deny the Bible and the person of Christ do not simply cry out for a new liberal theology. They also demand a new

morality. By a new morality they mean that we declare as
morally acceptable what the Bible declares is morally wrong.
They want us to turn from the truth delivered in the Bible concerning moral standards that should characterize Christians to
permit that which the Bible forbids. Moral apostasy always
follows theological apostasy. This is the logical and natural
order.

In 2 Peter 3, apostasy as it relates to the second coming of
Christ is predicted. Peter quotes the scoffers as saying, "Where
is the promise of his coming?" (v. 4). He goes on to state their
argument that the world has gone on for many centuries since
God created it, without any miraculous intervention in nature.
Therefore, nothing as miraculous as the second coming of
Christ can occur in the future.

The problem with these apostates is that those who take the
position that Christ is not coming again also logically take the
position that He did not come the first time. In other words,
their problem is not the second coming of Christ. Their problem is actually that they deny He came the first time as the
Scriptures indicate, born of a virgin, the God-man, the incarnate Son of God who died upon a cross for our sins and rose in
triumph from the grave.

The Scriptures are quite clear in stating that the professing
church will be apostate. In spite of the fact that many believers
in Christ form the body of Christ, Christians must face the
reality that the Scriptures are already being fulfilled, the last
days of the Church are already here.

One of these days a dramatic event will take place. We call
it the rapture of the Church, the catching up of the body of
Christ from among the professing church. Many believe this is
very near, that multiplied signs in the world and in God's dealings with Israel, as well as in God's dealings with the Church,
anticipate this event.

Obviously, when the rapture takes place, it will have a dramatic effect upon the professing church. Suddenly the presence

of those who have maintained a true testimony for God in the midst of the church at large, which has departed from the faith, will suddenly be removed. All that will be left of the professing church will be the unsaved who do not know Christ in a real way. Of course, this is a radical change of situation.

The question is sometimes raised, "Will the Church go through the tribulation?" It is my opinion that the Church will not; the true Church is raptured first. But it is also clear that the apostate church will go into the tribulation. In other words, those who have made a profession without reality will indeed move into the end time to be a part of the dramatic events that bring to a climax the period between the first coming of Christ and His second coming to set up His millennial Kingdom.

The period between the rapture of the Church and the time that Christ comes back to set up His Kingdom is the subject of extensive prophecy. These prophecies relate to all three major areas: the world in general, Israel, and the professing church. The professing church must be viewed in the context of the major events which form a part of this period.

Many believe when the rapture of the Church takes place there will emerge in the Middle East a revival of the ancient Roman Empire by ten countries banded together in the Mediterranean area. Out of these ten countries will emerge a dictator who will unite them and become the political strong man of the Middle East. When he gains this power, he will attempt to solve the problem of the controversy between Israel and the nations by entering into a covenant with Israel, described in Daniel 9:27. While the details of the covenant are not given, apparently it is a covenant of peace and protection. He offers to Israel his power as their security for peace for a period of seven years.

The Scriptures indicate that this future dictator keeps this period of peace for three and a half years; then he breaks the covenant and becomes Israel's persecutor instead of protector. This introduces the period of Israel's persecution for another three and a half years, which will climax with the second coming of Christ.

The last three and a half years preceding Christ's coming to set up His Kingdom is the Great Tribulation, predicted by Daniel in those express words in Daniel 12:1, and predicted in Jeremiah 30:3-11, speaking of the time of Jacob's trouble, a time of unprecedented evil. It is what Christ referred to as "great tribulation" in Matthew 24:15-22. It is the time of wrath and great tribulation of which the book of Revelation speaks; the time of unprecedented trouble when God will pour out great catastrophes on the world. Israel will be caught between opposing forces, with two out of three of them perishing in the land. During this period God will bring nations into judgment.

While the period of three and a half years will be characterized politically as a time of world government headed by this ruler in the Middle East, it will end in a gigantic world war, as segments of the world begin to contend with the world ruler for power. When Christ comes back in power and glory, there will be a great world war under way. He will resolve it by judging the nations and their armies and bringing in His kingdom.

In this context, what does the Scripture teach concerning the progress of the professing church? In the period between the rapture and the second coming of Christ to set up His kingdom, there are two distinct phases from the standpoint of the professing church. The first is the world-church phase.

It is significant in our twentieth century that there is a distinct movement toward a world church. It is all the more amazing because, in the history óf the church from the first century until now, the whole trend has been to more and more division.

First of all, there was a major division between the Eastern and Western churches which constituted the Greek Orthodox Church in the East and the Roman Catholic Church in the West. This took place in the eleventh century. The Protestant

Reformation introduced a third major element in Christendom, to divide the church into three major categories.

With the coming of the Protestant movement, there have been literally hundreds of subdivisions or denominations within Protestantism. In addition, in our twentieth century, literally thousands of churches have no affiliation whatever, operating as independent churches. The whole trend until our day has been to division and more division.

Then the world-church movement began. Beginning in 1925, a series of meetings were held to see if there could be some basis on which churches could unite. In 1938, The Temporary Ecumenical Council formed. In 1948, in Amsterdam, it was formalized, and a world organization was born. Its express purpose: to bring all Christendom into one, great, superchurch.

This world organization has not prospered. It has had many problems, especially in recent days. Evangelical Christians for the most part, and evangelical denominations, remained aloof of the ecumenical movement. One thing should be obvious, however. When the rapture of the Church takes place and true Christians are suddenly taken out of the world, a radically new situation will arise.

With true Christians gone, the Scriptures indicate the world church will achieve its goal. It will gather within its fold all forces of Christendom, all three major divisions of the church today and possibly some non-Christian religions. They will join together in one superchurch.

A picture in symbolic form is in Revelation 17, where a wicked woman is seated upon a scarlet-colored beast. It is a picture of religion riding triumphantly in combination with the political power of that time, the revived Roman Empire. In Revelation, John records he was carried away in the spirit into the wilderness:

> And I saw a woman sit upon a scarlet colored beast, full of the names of blasphemy, having seven heads and ten horns.

> And the woman was arrayed in purple and scarlet color and decked with gold and precious stones and pearls, having a golden cup in her hand full of abominations and filthiness of her fornication: And upon her forehead was a name written, MYSTERY, BABYLON THE GREAT, THE MOTHER OF HARLOTS AND THE ABOMINATIONS OF THE EARTH. And I saw the woman drunken with the blood of the saints and with the blood of the martyrs of Jesus: and when I saw her, I wondered with great admiration (Rev 17:3-6).

Expositors from the time of the Protestant Reformation have identified this woman as a symbol of apostate Christendom. She is described as seated upon a beast, a scarlet colored beast, having seven heads and ten horns. In Revelation 13, this beast is representative of the revived Roman Empire. It is the political power of that day. The woman who represents the religious power is astride the beast.

This posture indicates the beast supports her, and that she, to some extent, guides the beast. It also indicates that in the early period—possibly when Israel is at peace after the covenant is signed—the world church will come to power. And there will be a combined effort between the political and the religious forces of that day to pool their power and gain control over the entire world.

In Revelation 17:1, the woman sits upon many waters, which in verse 15 represent peoples, multitudes, nations, and tongues. In other words, she is the symbolic representation of a world religion, the ultimate in world church objectives. But it is a church entirely devoid of any redeeming feature that relates to biblical Christianity. This is reflected by the fact that the apostate church martyrs those who trust Christ in these sad days.

Revelation 17:16 introduces dramatic development. The ten horns of the beast, representing kings, hate the harlot, make her desolate and naked, eat her flesh, and burn her with fire.

They give their kingdom unto the beast. How can this dramatic development be understood?

It reveals that in the course of events this woman, who represents the world church, will be destroyed by the political power which formerly supported her. According to other Scriptures, this ruler in the Mediterranean at the mid-point of the seven-year period leading up to the second coming of Christ, comes to the point where he breaks his covenant with Israel. At that time he not only assumes universal political power—fulfilling Revelation 13:7, where he is declared to rule over every kindred, tongue, and nation—but he also takes over all the religions and all the money of the world. No one can buy or sell without his permission (Rev 13:17). He demands that everyone worship him on pain of death (Rev 13:15).

Here is the ultimate in apostasy, for this world ruler is Satan's substitute for Jesus Christ; he is Satan's nomination for king of kings and lord of lords, the substitute for Christ and His Kingdom. When this man reaches his supreme place of power, aided by Satan himself, he destroys the world church, which apparently has helped him reach this place of power. And in place of all the religions of the world he attempts to exalt himself as god, as an object of worship.

It is clear from Scripture that this man is Satan possessed. He is an atheist and blasphemes any kind of faith in God or Jesus Christ. He puts to death thousands of those who have turned to Christ. According to Revelation 7:9 there is a multitude in heaven which no man can number, of every kindred, tongue, and nation. When the origin of this multitude is questioned, the answer is given, "These are they which came out of great tribulation and have washed their robes, and made them white in the blood of the Lamb" (Rev 7:14). They are martyred dead of this awful time of great tribulation.

The final form of world religion will be the worship of this world dictator. Many see in the world church movement a preparation for the woman, symbol of the world church.

It is also rather amazing that during our twentieth century there has come into existence what we call Communism. Communism is generally recognized as a political ideology, imposed on the world largely through Russian influence. With amazing speed it has conquered almost one-third of the world's population. It is built upon the idea that wealth should be in the hands of the people, but all this is mostly words. Actually it is a means by which a few can control an entire nation.

Along with their political ideology comes a complete denial of Christianity and any form of religion that recognizes the supernatural or the existence of God. Russia and the communist nations banded with her in ideology afford the spectacle for the first time in history of nations who have officially espoused atheism.

Pagan nations of the past, while they were far from Christian truth, had some sort of a god. They may have worshiped some creature, the sun, moon, stars, or demons, but they had some kind of supernatural deity. A strange, new situation exists in the world now, where a major part of the world holds the belief that there is no God, that man is just an animal, that there is no life after death, and that there is no supernatural power in the world, nothing greater than man himself. This will be the "theology," if we may speak of it in this way, of the final form of world religion.

In the providence of God, Communism has been permitted in our world, not for its political ideology, which seems to fade from the scene as we follow the fulfillment of prophecy, but for its preparation of the world for the final world religion. Communism has served to condition millions of young people in our day in communist lands to accept the concept that there is no God, the only power is material or military, and there is no supernatural power in the world. All this has been permitted to prepare the world to move to the predicted climax revealed in the Scriptures—the climax of religion as dominated by Satan in his attempt to foist upon the world a substitute for faith in God, the Scriptures, and Jesus Christ.

As we contemplate the truth of the last days of the church on earth, it falls into three major phases. The first phase is, to a large extent, already fulfilled. This phase includes theological apostasy, or departing from the doctrine of the Bible as the Word of God, that Jesus Christ is the incarnate Son of God, that Christ died on the cross for our sin, that He rose again, that He is coming again to the earth. These are great fundamentals of the faith. To a large extent, in our theological schools and in our churches there has already been a fulfillment of theological apostasy.

In the last days of the church on earth, moral apostasy or departure from moral standards as laid down in the Word of God is predicted. Along with this will be the question of the skeptic, "Where is the promise of Christ's second coming?" It is a denial that Christ is coming to judge the world in righteousness and to set up His Kingdom. All of this is a part of our present situation, the first phase of predicted apostasy.

Events will come dramatically to a climax when the Lord comes for His Church and the Church is raptured out of the world and leaves behind a professing church completely devoid of any redeeming feature. After the rapture of the Church, the professing church will move on into the second great phase, the phase of the apostate world church symbolized in Revelation 17 and other Scriptures that allude to the same subject. The whole movement toward a world church as it has begun today will have its climax in this church after the true church has been raptured.

The third and final phase will begin when the world church is destroyed. The final form of religion will be completely apostate, and will have as the object of its worship the world ruler who is Satan's man, the Antichrist as some refer to him; he will be in place of Christ; he will be against Christ; he will be a blasphemer. He will cause those who trust Christ to be martyred for their faith. Here is the final climax of apostasy which began before human history in the fall of Satan, entered the human race in Eden, and will finally be judged by Jesus Christ when He comes in power from heaven.

The very fact that we live in a time when the first phase of apostasy has been already completed, and when the second phase cannot come until the rapture of the Church takes place, makes the imminence of the rapture clear. Preparations for both the second phase, the movement toward a world church, and the third phase, the movement toward atheism as the final form of religion, are already present in preliminary form. These facts added together constitute an impressive reminder that the time may be very near when Jesus Christ will come back in glory from heaven and fulfill the prophecies that relate to the Church. Then the other end-time events will rapidly move to their conclusion in the second coming of Jesus Christ in power to the earth when He comes to set up His Kingdom and reign in righteousness and peace upon the earth.

As we contemplate our present world the conclusion follows that we are indeed in the last days of the true Church on earth; and in the days when the church is in its predicted form of apostasy and departure from God. The coming of our Lord may be very near. While, from a theological standpoint, it has always been true that Christ could come at any time, today it is not simply that He *could* come.

The evidence accumulates that there is a great probability Christ may be coming very soon. As He comes, we should face the question of whether we are ready because we have placed our trust in Christ, and because day by day we live in expectation of that blessed hope and glorious appearing of our Lord Jesus Christ.

2

The Rapture of the Church:
How and When?

CHARLES LEE FEINBERG

ANY TREATMENT of the biblical doctrine of the Church without attention to the rapture is like an unfinished building, worse
than an unfinished symphony, and like history without a consummation. The doctrine of the rapture of the Church is the
necessary capstone to the teaching of the Scriptures on the
body of Christ. We must not seek the data for this truth in the
Old Testament, because even in Christ's day He spoke of the
building of the Church as a matter yet future to His time (Mt
16:18).

Furthermore, there could be no New Testament Church until
Christ in resurrection became the Head (Eph 1:15-23). Un-
fortunately, at this late hour in the history of the church we
still need to clarify what is meant by the word *Church*. Obviously, the reference is not to a physical or material structure,
nor to a sect, nor even a denomination. By the term we mean
that body of individuals who have placed faith in the Lord Jesus
Christ as Saviour from sin in this age of the fullness of grace.

The rapture of the Church is taught in a number of New
Testament passages. Its teaching is so clear and foundational

that without a proper understanding of it, the entire doctrine of the Church will be misunderstood. In fact, the New Testament will be all out of focus in this vital area. Because of space limitations we can only hit the highlights in the passages which are *prophecies of the rapture*. The order we follow is not that of the original proclamation of the passages, but as they are found in our Bibles, the order of the canon. The first passage is found in John:

> Let not your heart be troubled; ye believe in God, believe also in me. In my Father's house are many mansions; if it were not so, I would have told you. I go to prepare a place for you. And if I go and prepare a place for you, I will come again, and receive you unto myself, that where I am, there ye may be also (Jn 14:1-3).

Is it not sad this comforting passage is heard mostly at funerals! We must not allow ourselves to be robbed of these portions at any time.

In the first verse the Lord addresses the depression of the disciples. What had occasioned it? At the end of chapter 13, Peter had protested his undying fealty to Christ, and the Saviour had to warn him of his coming denial of the Redeemer he had come to love and follow. You can imagine the deep pall on the hearts of the apostolic band. Now the Saviour informs them He did not intend for their hearts to be weighed down with sorrow. He wants them to have joy, and in full measure. He commands them not to be agitated in mind and heart.

Our day witnesses a greater manifestation of troubled hearts and spirits than probably any other generation. Psychiatrists, psychologists, counselors, both secular and pastoral, are unable to cope with the great backlog of those who need help. It is one thing to command an untroubled heart, but how is it to be achieved? The Lord immediately states the method. The antidote is faith in God. That will lift up the spirit, stabilize the heart, and settle the mind.

But Christ adds more. Amazingly, He states that as they believe in God, they are to believe in Him. Was there ever a more direct and unequivocal statement of His deity? Yet many students of the New Testament tell us Christ never claimed to be God. How is that possible in the light of this verse? Mind you, too, He is addressing the world's firmest monotheists, yet He charges them that as they believe in the Lord God of Israel, they are to believe in Him. Here is the cure for depression.

Then the Lord speaks of the preparation He will inaugurate for His own for their eternal abode. He has bidden them believe. But believe what? There must be substance and object in one's faith. Upon what is it to be based? It cannot be pinned to thin air. It is founded on the reality of the Father's house and Christ's preparation for the coming of His Bride to live with Him. When Christ spoke these words, a visible temple was still in Jerusalem. But He is not referring to that as the Father's house. It was not the temple on earth, but in heaven. In Numbers 10 the Ark went before Israel in the wilderness to search them out a resting place. What the Ark did for them, the presence and activity of Christ accomplish for us in heaven.

We have learned there is an antidote for heart depression through faith in God and Christ, and that Christ prepares a new home for the heavenly Bride. Now Christ announces His return for His own. We know He has gone. Faith has taught us that He is making preparations for the wedding day and the ages beyond. But where does the Bride enter the scene? Christ will come in His resurrection glory to take His Bride to Himself and escort her to His and her eternal home, never to be parted.

A word of caution here. So many errors in the doctrine of the rapture arise from the fact that some think the rapture is a reward. It is not; it is all grace as the Bridegroom takes His Bride home. You may think by this time the passage certainly gives only a general overview. Yes, but it is the necessary framework into which other details will fit

Of what groups will the Bride consist? Part of the answer is given in 1 Corinthians 15:50-58:

> Now this I say, brethren, that flesh and blood cannot inherit the kingdom of God; neither doth corruption inherit incorruption. Behold, I show you a mystery; We shall not all sleep, but we shall all be changed, in a moment, in the twinkling of an eye, at the last trump: for the trumpet shall sound, and the dead shall be raised incorruptible, and we shall be changed. For this corruptible must put on incorruption, and this mortal must put on immortality. So, when this corruptible shall have put on incorruption, and this mortal shall have put on immortality, then shall be brought to pass the saying that is written, Death is swallowed up in victory. O death, where is thy sting? O grave, where is thy victory? The sting of death is sin; and the strength of sin is the law. But thanks be to God, which giveth us the victory through our Lord Jesus Christ. Therefore, my beloved brethren, be ye steadfast, unmovable, always abounding in the work of the Lord, forasmuch as ye know that your labour is not in vain in the Lord.

First, verses 50 and 53 state the divine principle. Paul speaks of the Kingdom in glory and those who will inherit it. He discloses the difference between the body, that is, the physical body, which is adapted to life on earth, and the body necessary for life in heaven. One will not suffice for the needs ahead, whereas the other is perfectly integrated into the surroundings of the heavenly realm. On earth the body needs renewal by blood, but not so with the heavenly body. That which is mortal and corruptible (subject to decay) fits the earthly scene, but not the heavenly.

Let us go back in the passage. Paul deals with two questions (v. 35): (1) How are the dead raised? He answers that death is but a sowing, and there will be a harvest. (2) What kind of body will they have? It will be a body like Christ's, beautifully portrayed in contrasting colors (vv. 40-44). Remember that a spiritual body is not an ethereal one. It is a physically resurrected body with the highest potential for the enjoyment of spiritual things.

Now the question comes: What will happen to the bodies of believers alive when the Lord returns? The answer is that these bodies will undergo a change in the rapture. It is a secret now made known (vv. 51-52) as to the change, the time involved, and the accompaniment of the event. In a moment, yes, even in a fraction of that time, it will take place to the sound of an announcing trumpet. Not all believers will undergo the experience of death. One generation will be immediately translated from the mortal state to the immortal in less time than it takes to tell it.

That change is absolutely necessary to provide the right type of body to enjoy eternity. In that hour, the victory of Christ at Calvary will be more fully revealed; His death will have robbed death and the grave of their prey. The death of Christ has made possible the rapture. (See Col 2:14-15; Heb 2:14-15; 1 Jn 3:8). In view of this revelation of truth, there is no need to remain in skepticism and doubt. The doctrine is eminently practical. Will it make the believer lazy and unfit for service on earth? No. Rather, it renders him ever abounding in work for the Lord, and that labor is not in vain as though there were no resurrection.

So far it has been revealed that living saints, who will be changed and translated, willl constitute part of that body spoken of by the Lord in John 14. But there is to be another component part of the Bride. We refer to saints that have gone to be with the Lord:

> But I would not have you to be ignorant, brethren, concerning them who are asleep, that ye sorrow not, even as others who have no hope. For if we believe that Jesus died and rose again, even so them also who sleep in Jesus will God bring with him. For this we say unto you by the word of the Lord, that we who are alive and remain unto the coming of the Lord shall not precede them who are asleep. For the Lord himself

shall descend from heaven with a shout, with the voice of
the archangel, and with the trump of God; and the dead in
Christ shall rise first; Then we who are alive and remain shall
be caught up together with them in the clouds, to meet the
Lord in the air; and so shall we ever be with the Lord. Wherefore, comfort one another with these words" (1 Th 4:13-18).

At the outset, Paul presents the reason for this disclosure.
He did not want Thessalonian believers, whose loved ones had
died since his visit to their city, in ignorance concerning departed saints. He reveals that it matters to God how believers
conduct themselves at the funeral of a child of God. They are
not to behave as unbelievers in the face of death. What is the
source of hope in such cases? The passage teaches that just
as Christ died and rose again, so will all His own, who have
died, rise and come with Him. The fears of the Thessalonians
were groundless. Could this be true? Paul says in effect, "I am
telling you God's truth."

Then the apostle elaborates on the theme. He assures griev-
ing ones they will not precede those who have departed. And
the program is outlined. First, the Lord Himself will return
with accompaniment and acclamation; King that He is, He will
be duly heralded in His coming for His own. Then, in order,
comes the resurrection of dead saints. Together with them
living saints will be caught up (raptured) in the clouds to the
rendezvous with the Lord in the air, a meeting that will never
know a separation. Here the apostle comforts us for our sojourn in this earthly sphere.

A Christian once visited in the home of a poor, afflicted believer in Dublin, Ireland. He tried to comfort the suffering one
with the words, "In My Father's house are many mansions."
"Stop a minute," said the dying but happy believer, "that is a
beautiful text, but there is one sweeter than it in the next verse:
'I will come again, and receive you unto Myself.' " Verily, it
will be the Lord Himself.

Since we have considered the prophecies of the rapture, let

us now turn to the *program of the rapture*. From the passages already treated, and others, we understand the rapture will be before the Great Tribulation which is to come on unbelieving Jew and Gentile. It will not be mid-Tribulation nor post-Tribulation. How do we know for certain? Two vital and determining facts enter here. First is the nature of the Church's hope. (See Phil 3:20-21; 1 Th 1:9-10; Titus 2:13; 1 Th 4:13-18, just considered.)

The hope of believers is seen—not as long life, nor painless death, nor wealth, nor world conversion—but as the return of the Lord for His own. It is no bright hope if the Tribulation must first intervene (cf. Lot in Gen 19:22). The epistles that speak of every phase of Christian life do not mention the Church's passing through this time. On the contrary, the promise is distinct that she will not (Rev 3:10).

Again, the nature of Daniel's seventy weeks in Daniel 9:24-27 shows that the Church cannot be on earth during this time of trial. These years are a unit in their reference to Israel, and Israel alone. The last period of seven years (the Tribulation time) cannot be torn apart. If God deals at that time with Israel as a nation, then the Church is not one of the groups on earth. If there is confusion here, the distinction between the Church and Israel is blurred.

As long as the Church is on earth, no Jew or Gentile can accept Christ as Saviour without entering the body of Christ (1 Co 12:13). If a saved remnant of Israel is in Jerusalem (Mt 24) and is still considered Israel and Judah, and if 144,000 (Rev 7) of Israel are saved (the seal of God is theirs), then why are they still counted as of Israel and not designated of the Church, if the Church is still on earth? If the Church were here, they would be part of it.

The rapture, moreover, will transpire in a moment (1 Co 15). It is not a long process like sanctification. Recall the catching away of Enoch and Elijah, two clear prefigurings of the rapture. It will not occur after some specified event. This is stated nowhere in Scripture. Finally, the rapture will take place for the entire Church as a body. The Bride will not be raptured in sections or parts. There will be only two classes simultaneously caught up: dead saints and living saints. Ephesians 5:25-27 indicates the Bride as a glorious Church, not a spotted or wrinkled one, let alone mutilated or fragmented.

Finally, it is imperative to view this doctrine in the light of *the practical value of the rapture*. Many assert that belief in this blessed hope (Titus 2:11-13) is a detriment to Christian life and service. Did it affect mighty men of God in other days in that fashion? Has it had that influence on some of the choice servants of God today? Let the facts speak for themselves. We are told this doctrine leads to pessimism. If it is pessimism, it is a Biblical one which does not look to mankind to cure the ills of humanity. As Capt. Reginald Wallis used to quote a motto from an optometrist's window in Dublin: "You can't be optimistic with a misty optic."

The Spirit of God must not have considered this truth a pessimistic one, for He relates it in the New Testament to practically every exhortation, whether it be to watchfulness, moderation, patience, practical sanctification, faithfulness in service, purity, endurance in trials, brotherly love, separation from worldly lusts, consolation in time of bereavement, and many others. Above all, it keeps the believer's eyes in the right direction—looking for the Lord!

When Shackleton, it is said, was driven back from his search for the South Pole, he left his men on Elephant Island and promised to come back to them. Working his way as best he could to South Georgia, he tried to get back to fulfill his promise, and failed; he tried again and failed. The ice was between him and the island. He was not able to return, but he could not rest. Though the season was wrong, and they told him repeatedly that it was impossible, yet he tried it again in his little boat. It was the wrong time of the year, but he got nearer the island. There was an open path between the sea and the place where he had left his men. He ran his boat in at the risk of being crushed, got all his men on board, and came out again before the ice crashed together. It all happened in half an hour.

When the excitement was partly over, he turned to one and said, "Well, you were certainly all packed and ready!" The man answered, "You see, boss, Wild (second in command) never gave up hope, and whenever the sea was at all clear of ice, he rolled up his sleeping-bag, and said to all the men, 'Roll up your sleeping-bags, boys; the boss may come today.'" A black outlook was suddenly changed, and they were all safe, bound for home.

Do we keep our hope bright? It is based on a surer word than ever man could utter. As believers, we must keep the hope warm and bright in our hearts. If you have never trusted Christ, this hope is not yours. Flee to Christ as Saviour from sin to make sure of a hope for eternity.

3

When Can the Church Expect the Lord's Return?

WENDELL G. JOHNSTON

RECALL SOME of the memorable events that have taken place in your lifetime. The country was exhilarated when Lindbergh crossed the Atlantic and came back to a hero's welcome. Television brings us many spectacular events. I watched Roger Bannister break the four-minute mile. I am amazed at what man can accomplish. In the past few years we sent a man to the moon. I remember those early shots when Alan Shepard went into space. Then John Glenn orbited the earth. It certainly was thrilling to see a rocket blast off into the blue sky. All the world marvelled when the first men went to the moon, and Neil Armstrong set his ship down on its surface saying, "The Eagle has landed."

As exciting as these events have been, the Word of God tells us that there is an event coming that is going to be even more exciting, and much more interesting—especially for those of us who know Jesus Christ as Saviour—than any past events. The Scripture says that Christ is coming back for His Church. We call it the rapture. At a time not known to us, we will be caught up to meet the Lord in the air. Great confusion will be

36

here on earth because suddenly, without any warning, thousands of people will be missing. People will panic because of this; some will understand exactly what is happening because they have heard the truth but have not believed it. There will be great tragedy here on earth. There will be great joy for those of us who see the Lord Jesus Christ. People all over the world will be affected.

When can the Church expect this spectacular event? The first thing to consider is that the coming of Christ for the Church is imminent, that is, it could be at any time. There are no events given to us in the Word of God that must be fulfilled before Christ can come back for His Church. In other words, it is the next prophetic event, as far as Scripture is concerned. The Lord taught this to His disciples in John 14.

Much of what we find in the epistles that we call Church truth has as its beginning the teachings Jesus gave in the gospels. It is possible to find almost all the teachings in the epistles in their seed form through the teachings of the Lord. For instance, in Matthew 16 Jesus said that He was going to build His Church, and the gates of hell would not prevail against it. The very beginning, actually the prophecy concerning the Church is there. He was going to build His Church. He had to die first of all, to be raised, to ascend into heaven to be at the right hand of the Father, and then to send the Spirit before the Church began.

There it is in seed form: "I will build my church." In the epistles this is expanded. As Paul tells us, here is a mystery not known in the Old Testament, that God is forming a "new man," from Jew and Gentile, placing them together in what is called the Church, the Body of Christ.

In John 15, Jesus speaks of the very close relationship believers have. He says, "Abide in me, and I in you." In the epistles, Paul talks about our being in Christ. The seed thought was there in John 15 concerning the union and communion we have with the Lord Jesus, before Christ ever left His disciples.

He said, "Abide," or, "Remain close to Me." Paul reveals the
wonderful privilege we have today of being in Christ. In the
gospels, John the Baptist said that Jesus would baptize with
the Holy Spirit. The Lord, before He ascended into heaven,
said the disciples would be baptized by the Holy Spirit not many
days hence. The baptism of the Spirit is not explained even in
the book of Acts. It is not until Paul's teaching in 1 Corinthians
12:13 that he explains what it means; we are placed into the
body of Christ. It was first mentioned in the gospels. The ministry of the Holy Spirit is given to us in the gospels by the Lord
Jesus (Jn 16). It is amplified and expanded in the epistles.

It is not unusual, then, that we should find the seed thoughts
concerning the coming of Christ for His Church in the gospels.
John 14 records the words of our Lord:

> Let not your heart be troubled: ye believe in God, believe also
> in me. In my Father's house are many mansions [or dwelling
> places]: if it were not so, I would have told you. I go to pre-
> pare a place for you. And if I go and prepare a place for you,
> I will come again and receive you unto myself; that where I
> am, there ye may be also (vv. 1-3).

Now, this is distinctly literal. He was going away; there is no
question that He literally went away. He went into the presence
of the Father, and He says, "I will come again." That is an interesting phrase because it is actually not in the future tense,
but in the present tense, "I come again." Being in the present
tense, it emphasizes the imminency of His coming: "I'm coming." That coming could be at any time.

He did not speak here of His coming for Israel, which is a
different subject, the one the Lord Jesus prophesied in Matthew 24 and 25, where He dealt specifically with Israel. On the
Mount of Olives, when Jesus was speaking to His disciples, they
asked: "Tell us, when shall these things be?" He had just
spoken about the destruction of Jerusalem and the Temple they
looked at from the Mount of Olives. Jesus told them it would
be torn down.

They said, "When shall these things be? and what shall be the sign of thy coming, and of the end of the world (Mt 24:3). This is a different subject altogether from the rapture of the Church. He is coming to establish the Kingdom at the end of that age. The Lord mentioned certain things that will take place, certain signs they should look for. He said, "When you see all these things, then you know the end of the age is near and the coming, My coming to establish the Kingdom, is nigh" (v. 33, paraphrased).

In John 14 the terminology is different. The disciples were concerned. The Lord had taught them concerning His death and resurrection, but they still did not understand. They were deeply moved and troubled. Jesus said, "I am going, but I am coming back for you. I come again." This is the certainty and the imminency of His coming.

In the epistles, Paul expands on the teachings of the Lord. In chronological order, the first passage is 1 Thessalonians 4:13-18. Paul enlarges on the seed thought Jesus gave His disciples, "I come again." He indicates the Lord Jesus is going to come, those who have died in Christ shall be raised, and those who are alive will be caught up together to meet Him in the air. Paul was speaking to people in the church at Thessalonica who were concerned about the Lord's coming. What happens to the loved ones who have died in Christ; how do they participate in this? Paul explains how.

In this teaching he also gives the concept that it is going to be very sudden. There is no time element given here; it is not after so many events, or when so many signs are fulfilled. It is suddenly the Lord comes back for His saints. Verse 17 reveals: "Then we which are alive and remain shall be caught up [this is where we get the word *rapture*] together with them in the clouds, to meet the Lord in the air: and so shall we ever be with the Lord." What a tremendous comfort to them! They would see their loved ones again as well as the Lord.

Chronologically, 1 Corinthians comes next. Paul again

picks up the subject of the Lord's return, emphasizing the suddenness of His coming: "Behold, I shew you a mystery; we shall not all sleep, but we shall all be changed, in a moment, in the twinkling of an eye, at the last trump: for the trumpet shall sound, and the dead shall be raised incorruptible, and we shall be changed" (1 Co 15:51-52). Paul says those who are dead will be raised, and those who are alive will be changed, to meet the Lord in the air. He is coming for us to receive us unto Himself, because He has gone to prepare a place for us.

The book of Philippians revolves around two of Paul's experiences. In chapter one he tells about his prison experience. In chapter three he talks about his conversion experience: what it meant to him and what happened on the Damascus road. He states he is anticipating resurrection from the dead. He uses the word used only here in the New Testament, "an out-resurrection from among the dead ones," meaning the rapture of the Church. He anticipates this.

Now he is at the end of his ministry; he is in Rome; he is a prisoner, but he still has this hope. The apostle Paul, still strong in faith and believing in the coming of the Lord, calls it the "blessed hope, and glorious appearing of our great God and Saviour Jesus Christ" (Titus 2:15). So the New Testament teaches the coming of Christ for the Church is imminent.

The second thing to consider is that the coming of the Lord for the Church will precede the Tribulation events. His coming for us will be before the time of tribulation to come upon the earth. Now, when you deal with a subject like this, it is easy to become emotionally involved. There are those who believe the Church will go through the tribulation; they become emotional about it; they talk about the purifying of the Church. There are those who believe the Church will not go through the tribulation, but again it is an emotional concept with them. We will be taken away from all the suffering, pain, decisions, and problems of this world. We want it to happen; therefore, we believe it will happen. It is necessary for us to look into the Word of God to find out what the Scripture has to say concerning this, because here are the authority and hope for our faith.

In 1 Thessalonians 3:10 Paul states the reason he wrote the epistle: "Night and day, praying exceedingly that we might see your face, and might perfect that which is lacking in your faith" that is, to supply what is lacking. He realized that believers in the church in Thessalonica had a need; they did not understand all the teachings Paul wanted them to comprehend.

There were things lacking in their faith, and that is why he wrote to them. He talks about their love, that it might increase. He speaks of holiness and sanctification. He writes of the coming of Christ for believers. These were important truths for the people to know and understand. When you come to 2 Thessalonians, again he is trying to correct, to supply what is needed. Because now there is another problem, one that had risen in the church over the matter of the Lord's return.

The answer comes in 2 Thessalonians 2: "Now we beseech you, brethren, by the coming of our Lord Jesus Christ, and by our gathering together unto him, That ye be not soon shaken in mind, or be troubled, neither by spirit, nor by word, nor by letter as from us, as that the day of Christ is at hand" (vv. 1-2). The phrase "day of Christ" is actually the "day of the Lord." The words "at hand" mean "present, already there." So it would read that "the day of the Lord is present, or already in existence."

Now here was the problem. After Paul had left and had written his first epistle, there were those who taught that the Day of the Lord, which would begin in tribulation or darkness, had already come. Paul wrote and besought them by the coming. The preposition "by" means for the benefit of, or on behalf of. This is the defense for the teaching that he calls "the coming of our Lord Jesus Christ and by our gathering together unto Him." The two phrases actually are one thought, the coming of our Lord Jesus Christ and our gathering together unto Him.

At the beginning of the chapter, Paul says that what he was teaching them was for the benefit of the truth of the Lord's return and our gathering together unto Him, which has to do with the rapture of the Church.

Then he indicated how the difficulty came into the church. He warned them not to be shaken by all this, or troubled, "neither by spirit," for there were those who said that the Holy Spirit had revealed this to them, that they were in the Tribulation. It is so easy for people to say that the Spirit has taught them something. "Nor by word," because some claimed that Paul told them when he was there. Paul said, "Don't believe it." "Nor by letter," some maintained they had an epistle, a private communication from the apostle himself. Paul was trying to correct all this.

The same problems Paul had in his day we certainly have in ours. People claim special revelation, and these things all need to be tested according to God's Word. So Paul said, "Don't let anyone deceive you by any means, because the day of the Lord is not present." He told them when they could expect the Day of the Lord to come. "Let no man deceive you by any means: for that day shall not come except there come a falling away first, and that man of sin be revealed, the son of perdition" (v. 3).

Paul declared there is going to be the apostasy. He emphasized it.

We know in our day there is apostasy; there is a falling away. People have turned away from the doctrine; they have turned from moral value. After the true Church has been taken, moral values will be completely gone; people will turn away from the worship of God or any gods. They will turn to atheism. Paul says there will be a great apostasy and he links it with Satan's man, the man of sin. This apostasy relates to the time when Satan will have his prince, his counterfeit for the Lord Jesus Christ, "who opposeth and exalteth himself above all that is called God, or that is worshipped; so that he as God sitteth in the temple of God, showing himself that he is God" (v. 4). Here is the ultimate in apostasy.

Paul was affirming the Day of the Lord was not present, because in the Day of the Lord the apostasy will come to fruition through the man of sin. Imagine what will happen on the earth when this is true, when this man sits in God's place in the holy Temple. Paul said, "Remember . . . that, when I was yet with you, I told you these things?' '(v. 5). He had already taught them concerning this, but they had to be reminded. He taught that the Day of the Lord cannot come, we should not expect it, until there is this apostasy, and the man of sin is revealed. Paul then explained why the Day of the Lord had not come:

> And now ye know that withholdeth (or restraineth), that he might be revealed in his time. For the mystery of iniquity doth already work: only he who now restraineth will restrain until he be taken out of the way. And then shall that wicked be revealed (vv.6-8).

Paul said the Day of the Lord will not come until there come great apostasy and the revelation of the man of sin. He also stated there was something withholding; this something he called a Person, "He who is restraining." Paul was not referring to the government. Grammatically, this is not possible. Aside from that, the government has never been able to restrain wickedness, especially spiritual wickedness, which would be brought in through the man of sin. This Restrainer has to be a divine Person, because only the power of God can restrain sin and wickedness. This fits the person of the Holy Spirit, whose ministry in this age is to convict of sin, righeousness, and judgment, as the Lord Jesus Christ taught in John 16. So Paul declared there is a restraining going on now, and this restraining is by a Person, the Spirit of God. Moreover, this restraining will continue until He be taken out of the way.

Now, in a unique way the Spirit of God, who was in the

world before Pentecost, came at Pentecost. The Scripture tells us that the Spirit was poured out as Peter preached to the people (Ac 2). Jesus promised that the Spirit would come. The Holy Spirit had been in the world, but He was to come in a special way. He would come and baptize those who believed. That did not take place in the Old Testament. The baptism of the Holy Spirit was a ministry begun at Pentecost. Also, the Spirit of God would indwell the believers, for Jesus said that the Spirit of God "dwelleth with you and shall be in you" (Jn 14:17). This was His particular and unique ministry, and has been since Pentecost; also the restraining of sin, by Himself and through believers who are on earth.

When He is taken out of the way, that is, when His ministry is complete by God's removal of believers from this earth, there will be no more baptizing of believers, even though people will be saved in the Tribulation. The Church began at Pentecost, and it will end at the rapture, the coming of the Lord for His Church. The indwelling, which was not true of the Old Testament, is valid in this age. When that unique ministry is completed, the Spirit of God will be taken out of the way, for God is going to remove believers from this earth. The Spirit will be in the world, just as He was before Pentecost, but the unique ministry of the Spirit will be finished. Now Paul says that after the Restrainer is gone, then shall that wicked one be revealed.

When will Christ come for His Church? He will come before the Day of the Lord, before the time of tribulation, before the man of sin is revealed. That event will take place when the Church is complete, when the last person has been baptized into the Body of Christ. When the last person has been indwelt by the Spirit of God, the Church will be removed, and the Spirit's unique ministry for this age will end. Think of what will happen on this earth when all Christians have left and the Spirit no longer works through the Church to fight evil. When Christians are gone, the great apostasy can come.

Consider one more thing: since the Lord will return before

the Tribulation, are there any indicators that the events which will take place in the Tribulation are beginning to appear? In spite of the fact there are no signs to be fulfilled before Christ comes for His Church, can we see shadows of future events? There are certain signs to take place before Christ comes for Israel, and certain things to look for during the time of tribulation.

Is it possible for us to see any of these things developing to help us understand the coming of the Lord for us is very near? Several things should be mentioned. The Scripture states in Daniel 2, 7, and Revelation 13, 17 that there will be in the end days during the Tribulation time a Western alliance of ten nations. Out of this will come the man of sin, the great Western ruler.

In our day nations gather together for economic reasons. The currency crisis may be another means to move these countries closer. We must realize that in the end time it will be for political reasons that they will be united. So we can see nations are forming a Western confederacy; this is not to say that what is forming now is the fulfillment of prophecy. It is interesting that there is an alliance even today. Revelation 17 speaks of a religious system which will be worldwide, a superchurch, an ecumenical church. We see a movement toward one world church.

A third thing I think important is the rise of Israel on the world scene. Since 1948 Israel has been gaining in power; she becomes more important each day. The Bible prophesies this will happen. As you read through the prophetic messages in the Old Testament, you find the importance of Israel. In 1967, the Six-Day War confirmed that Israel is a strong nation. We should expect Israel will be more important each day, in view of what Scripture reveals concerning the end times.

It is interesting also that Russia aligns herself with Israel's enemies, particularly the Arab nations. Ezekiel prophesies Russia in conflict with Israel during the Tribulation. In Isaiah

19:24 we read that Egypt will also come to prominence in the last days. In recent months Egypt has become very independent, shaking herself free even of Russia. This was a significant development in 1972. Isaiah says Egypt is going to be an independent, important nation in those last days.

All indicators lead us to believe the rapture of the Church is near. How should we respond? Paul wrote to Titus:

> For the grace of God that bringeth salvation hath appeared to all men, teaching us that denying ungodliness and worldly lusts, we should live soberly, righteously, and godly in this present world; looking for that blessed hope, and the glorious appearing of the great God and our Saviour Jesus Christ; who gave himself for us, that he might redeem us from all iniquity, and purify unto himself a peculiar people, zealous of good works (2:11-14).

Paul says several important things here. The truth of the Lord's return should have a sobering effect on us because many are still lost. We may be the only witness that people will hear or see because they may watch us more than listen to us. It should challenge us to holiness, to purify ourselves. Second, Paul states we should be looking for that blessed hope. Our eyes should be heavenward. We are not looking for signs now; we look for Christ Himself. When Paul declared in Philippians 1:21, "For to me to live is Christ and to die is gain," he wanted to be with Christ. Finally, we should be busy serving the Lord, zealous of good works, and doing what God wants us to do.

4

The Spread of the Occult

HAL LINDSAY

THESE ARE EXCITING TIMES. And I feel that since writing *The Late Great Planet Earth*, many things have developed. I can concentrate on only one now. But as we look at the precise pattern of events predicted hundreds of years ago by the Hebrew prophets, we see Israel back in the land; they have reconquered old Jerusalem, and for the first time in 2,600 years they have maintained a sovereign possession and rulership of Jerusalem.

Already they have spotted the exact foundation of where the Temple was before Titus destroyed it in A.D. 70. In Israel, I went underneath the wall into a locked area where secret excavations are going on, where few Israelites are allowed. I stood within ten meters of where the Holy of Holies is said to have stood. There is much interest in building something there.

Another thing we see is that the Middle East has become even more the focus of the world. I mentioned the strategic importance of the Middle East in *The Late Great Planet Earth;* but how much more prominent has it become now because of the energy crisis. The fact that most of the known oil reserves in the world are in the Arab countries means the Arabs are going to use it to bring pressure upon Israel.

We see the Arabs more united, and their confederacy is in great hostility against Israel. Actually, their attack on Israel in the future will launch the last war of the world. The stage is now being set in the Middle East. The Russians have become even more the enemy of Israel. In the West is the continued development of what I believe is the revival of the Roman Empire, as predicted by Daniel and the book of Revelation. There will be a ten-nation confederacy rise out of the ruins of the Roman culture and become the greatest power on earth in the last days. Since writing the book there are now three more nations in that union, nine in all.

We see the East become even more a piece of this prophetic puzzle. A recent *U. S. News and World Report* announced that Red China now has not only nuclear weapons, but also the ability to deliver hydrogen warheads upon Moscow and targets all through the East and Middle East. Within a few years they will have the ability to put missiles on continental United States. The Red Chinese are capable of fielding an army of 200,000,000, as predicted in Revelation 9:16.

We see these things continue to develop. But there is something that has literally exploded in our world, and I want to focus on it now. Around 1967 and 1968 I began to notice unusual changes on the college campus and among youth. I began to find those who had been in the radical movement, intellectuals, youth leaders, college students, beginning to accept the supernatural. Most of these had been agnostics and atheists. College professors who were in radical politics about 1970 began to be involved in witchcraft, the occult, parapsychology, ESP, and so forth. So now there has been virtually a reverse in thinking.

Before the late sixties, the average college student and professor were skeptical of the supernatural. What we see now is unprecedented in history. People who went through an age of rationalism for nearly two centuries (it started with the Renaissance) saw the age of rationalism do away with the supernatural and its credibility. Faith in the Bible as a reliable document was attacked, so that today on the college campus this Book is ridiculed and maligned in most classrooms. There was virtually an age of antisupernaturalism, but this age ended around 1967 and 1968. You and I live in what can be called an age of supernaturalism. A tremendous battle begins to take shape, a confrontation in the spiritual realm. The lines are being drawn. And I don't believe very many Christians realize how violent this battle may become. In *Newsweek,* April 9, 1973, in the education department, it was stated:

> There may be more than meets the eye to the eerie silence on the nation's college campuses these days. Some of the very same students who were once embroiled in activistic causes are now turning out reality in favor of the supernatural. In response, courses in a wide variety of occult subjects are now among the most popular additions to the curriculum at many schools.

I have been travelling on college campuses for at least fifteen years. And I tell you, the occult is now one of the biggest things on the college campus. Departments, added with the name *parapsychology,* in many cases are out and out experiments in the occult. The *Newsweek* article went on to say:

> Fascination with the supernatural is very much a part of the counterculture's reaction against the rationalistic, scientific tradition of the post-Renaissance Western thought. One professor goes on to say, "Social upheaval has produced increased interest in the supernatural. The occult represents a response to the breakdown of society, the sense of powerlessness of individuals to control their own destiny."

Students sense a powerlessness to control their destiny. They feel swamped by materialism, but they have no way to escape it. Underneath the quiet surface is a seething cauldron of the occult. Now, there are other articles which indicate how deeply the occult touches our society. An article from May 13, 1973,

Los Angeles Times is entitled "Psychic Group Conducts Research to Dispel Any Image of Witchcraft." The group is called the Southern California Society for Psychical Research, Inc. They have a scientific advisory committee, and its researchers tend to be professional people—physicians, psychiatrists, physicists, physiologists, and social workers. I quote:

> High volume tape recordings are used to capture what are said to be faint voices of the dead, communicating from the spirit world. Photographs carefully studied yield images and insights that weren't visible when the pictures were taken. Controlled experimentation attempts to determine if psychical healings take place, and what physiological changes occur as a part of the process.

This scientific investigation board is going into the occult, into many of these things, and they are establishing scientifically that supernatural things are happening. And they have actually recorded voices in seances that were of spirits, talking and imitating the departed dead. The Bible teaches that contacts can be made with the spirit world, but they are contacts with demons who impersonate dead people. This is one of Satan's ways of misleading people who are trying to reach out to the supernatural. Overemotional people and those who long for loved ones who have died are gullible in seances. There are plenty of supernatural phenomena, and they are from Satan.

Another indication of how the occult touches our society is seen in some of our best sellers. Among some of the best sellers are the writings of Jeane Dixon, the writings of Ruth Montgomery, and the all-time best seller, *Jonathan Livingstone Seagull*. This book was advertised in *Christian Book Seller* magazine, of all places. It is now being read as a part of the curricula of many schools; it is being given away by some of the major savings-and-loans groups in California. In the *National Enquirer,* February 4, 1973, author Richard Bach tells where he obtained his material. I quote:

"I was walking home one night when I heard a voice say very calmly, Jonathan Livingstone Seagull. I looked around, but there was no one there. I ran all the way home and locked the door behind me. I sat on the edge of the bed, scared and bewildered. I knew this all meant something, but what it meant I just had no idea." After a few seconds of silence, the vision of a seagull materialized in his room and began telling him the story of Jonathan, which he recorded on his typewriter, said Bach. "But the vision disappeared before the tale was finished, and it wasn't until eight years later, in 1967, that the voice returned to complete the story. The vision and the voice were there again, and so was Jonathan Livingstone Seagull, flying along, talking to me, resuming his story where he had left off eight years previously." Bach, who has written three other books, said that when people refuse to believe his story of how the novel was written, he points out that the style of writing is "just not mine."

Now, this was dictated by a demon, and you can discern within it things that are absolutely anti-Christ. It gives the idea that whether there is a heaven or a hell is irrelevant, and so on. Another popular series of books have been written by a Carlos Casteniadas, Ph. D., of U. C. L. A. All of his books are best sellers, and they will tell you how to become a sorcerer. *Time,* March 5, 1973 stated:

A sorcerer's power, Casteniadas insists, is unimaginable, but the extent to which a sorcerer's apprentice can hope to use it is determined by, among other things, the degree of commitment. The full use of power can only be acquired with the help of an ally spirit, which attaches itself to the student as a guide.

Demon possession is what I am talking about. I have confronted it many times in the last three years. It seems when I began to write *Satan Is Alive and Well On Planet Earth,* I was confronted with all kinds of things that, if I did not know Jesus Christ, would have scared me to death. But in the name of

Jesus Christ, I have commanded these spirits to come out of people, and they have come out.

Another indication of where we are in this tremendous resurgence of the power of the occult is taken from *Esquire,* April, 1973. The article is called, "An Occult Guide to the Stock Market." T. O. Tully has amassed a fortune through what he says is the use of ESP in predicting the market. Another one is Mrs. Dora Lee, who has attributed all of her fantastic gains in the stock market to her husband. The only problem is, he has been dead for more than ten years. She has contacted him in a seance, and he tells her when to sell and when to buy. An upper-Manhattan occult group invests as a group and then casts spells upon the market.

The Scripture warns us about involvement in the occult and what happens when a society becomes involved in it. Deuteronomy 18:9-12 tells us it is an abomination to the Lord for anyone to be involved in any form of the occult: "When you enter the land which the Lord your God gives you, you shall not learn to imitate the detestable things of those nations. There shall not be found among you anyone who makes his son or his daughter pass through the fire" (vv. 9-10, NASB).

This referred to the practice of offering children as sacrifices to heathen gods, especially the heathen god Molech. They would stab them with a knife and burn them alive. It is inevitable; when a society gets involved in the occult the result will be human sacrifice.

It was reported in the *Los Angeles Times,* May 3, 1973: "A seventeen-year-old change boy in a pin-ball arcade was strapped to a table and tortured for a day before being murdered by a group of young Satan worshippers as a sacrifice, police say."

This happened at Daytona Beach. These sorts of things will result when people get too deeply into the occult—and this includes all forms.

Divination is also dangerous for a Christian. Scripture goes on to say:

> Or one who practices witchcraft, or one who interprets omens, or a sorcerer, or one who casts a spell, or a medium, or a spiritist, or one who calls up the dead. For whoever does these things is detestable to the Lord; and because of these detestable things, the Lord your God will drive them out before you (vv. 11-12, NASB).

It is amazing how the occult is particularly intriguing to the intelligent, the academic community. Now, what is the significance? I believe it has a prophetic significance. Consider Matthew 24:24. Do not be intimidated by what is going on around you, but be alert to conditions about you. Matthew states there would be something that would begin to be the mood of the world before Christ returns. "For false Messiahs and false prophets will arise and will show great signs and wonders so as to mislead, if possible, even the elect."

These false prophets and false Messiahs in the power of Satan would show these things. 2 Thessalonians 2:9-11 reads: "That is, the one whose coming is in accord with the activity of Satan, with all power and signs and false wonders."

Revelation 13 adds: "The whole world will worship him, and the dragon." The dragon is explained in Revelation 12:9 as Satan. In other words, there is coming a whole world of Satan worshipers who will worship a man who claims to be God. Now, that could happen today, as berserk as this world is. It still could happen at this moment, but the way is being prepared for it through this explosion of the occult.

Do you know where the leading experimentation in the occult is going on today? The leader of the world in exploring the occult is Soviet Russia. What is coming will be satanic miracles, powers, signs, and lying wonders. The world which has rejected this Book as the criterion to judge the supernatural has no way to discern the source of the miracles that are going to be poured out through these occultic people. The way is being prepared for world thinking apart from Christ to receive the supernatural through occult power. Now, what is the significance? "And with all the deception of wickedness for those who perish, because they did not receive the love of the truth so as to be saved" (2 Th 2:10, NASB).

People who didn't receive the love of the truth will be deceived. And again: "For this reason God will send upon them a deluding influence so that they might believe what is false" (v. 11).

Today it is either receive what God has said through the truth, or else be in for the great deception. Do not mistake it, that deception is coming. But where will the world go? Where is it headed? Look at the conditions describing the world of the future in Revelation 9:20. This verse describes all men without Christ in the last period of world history before He personally comes back to this earth to straighten it out. Here is the attitude of man after some awesome judgments have fallen on the earth: "And the rest of mankind who were not killed by these plagues did not repent of the works of their hands, so as not to worship demons" (v. 20).

The world of the future will worship demons. And I believe the occult will merge with false religion, even with many who claim to be Christians. We're told in Revelation 13 a false prophet is coming: "He deceives those who dwell on the earth because of the signs which it was given him to perform in the presence of the beast" (v. 14). The beast is the Roman dictator, the one who is coming in Europe.

> Telling those who dwell on the earth to make an image to the beast, who had the wound of the sword and has come to life. And there was given to him to give breath to the image of the beast, that the image of the beast might even speak and cause as many as do not worship the image of the beast to be killed. And he causes all, the small and the great, and the rich and the poor, the free men and the slaves, to be given a mark on their right hand, or on their forehead (vv. 15-16, NASB).

The world is preparing for this great false prophet to come. And he will convince the world to worship this great political, religious ruler who will rise up in the future in the Middle East.

Prophecy continues to keep coming together and fitting into the pattern exactly as it was predicted hundreds of years ago. It is thrilling to know Jesus Christ personally. The only way to contact the supernatural, and for it to become a life-changing experience, is to see that nearly 2,000 years ago Jesus Christ came down to this earth and became a Man so that, as a perfect Man, He might die for all other men. Because He had no sin of His own, He could take the guilt for our sins upon Himself. When Jesus cried, "My God, My God, why hast Thou forsaken me?" it was because in that awful moment He bore the wrath of a holy God against rebellious men. He died in your place so that you could be given eternal life.

Once you receive Him, you can know the supernatural. And we can touch the invisible; the Spirit of God can make us understand this Book, the supernatural.

The great moment when all of our hopes will be realized is near, and Christ shall descend from heaven with a shout and the voice of the archangel. Paul said the great mystery was that there would be a generation who would never know what it was to die physically. Are you living in the light of such a hope? Are you, right now, living your life in such a way that you will be glad to see Jesus face to face?

The Glorious Destiny of Believers

S. MAXWELL CODER

IT HAS OFTEN BEEN my privilege to examine missionary candidates in the field of Bible doctrine. Even some who have attended good schools give very curious answers to questions about the destiny of believers. They argue that Adam and Abraham were Christians, and that we shall all join them in one great family in heaven, made up of the people of Israel, the Church, and all other saved persons. They are unaware that the Church is a mystery kept secret since the world began (Ro 16:25), with a place in the divine program quite different from that of Israel.

Some are even convinced Christians will be on earth during the Tribulation, hiding themselves with everyone else in the dens and rocks of the mountains as they experience the great day of the wrath of the Lamb (Rev 6:15-17). Since people with specialized training for missions sometimes have only a vague understanding of what is ahead for Christians, a survey of this whole field of revelation is an appropriate subject of Bible study.

WHAT HAPPENS TO BELIEVERS AT DEATH

A satisfying revelation has been given to us about believers who are now absent from the body and present with the Lord (2 Co 5:8). At the moment they close their eyes in death they open them in the presence of the Lord in glory. Only momentarily will they be in the valley of the shadow of death. Many years ago I was driving with my family when a truck passed us, going the other way, and its shadow passed over us. I said, "How much better it is to be run over by the shadow of a truck than by the truck itself." It is in that dark valley of the shadow that our loved ones discover the Lord is at their side, so they are able to say, "Thou art with me" (Ps 23:4).

When Stephen was stoned to death, "he fell asleep" (Ac 7:60). That word is never used of the human soul or spirit. Only the body sleeps. The early Christians were aware of this. They called the place where they laid their loved ones a cemetery, which means a sleeping place, and we still use their word today. They knew the body without the spirit is dead (Ja 2:26), but that the angels may carry the spirits of our loved ones to the presence of the Lord after their bodies fall asleep (Lk 16:22).

They knew a great deal more than this. In His presence is fulness of joy (Ps 16:11). It is far better for them to be with Him than here with us in the land of the dying, for they are in the land of the living (Phil 1:21-23). The separation is only temporary, because any day may bring the fulfillment of the promise the Lord will receive all of us unto Himself, when He descends from heaven with a shout, with the voice of the archangel, and with the trump of God. That is the moment in which we shall see our loved ones again.

Knowing these revealed truths makes heaven nearer and dearer. And it provides the greatest source of comfort for the sorrowing to be found in the Bible. We are told to comfort one another with these words. There are comfort, blessing, and understanding awaiting us in every word written about our future.

What Happens at the Rapture

Several things are revealed in 1 Thessalonians 4:13-18 that are instructive. The Lord descends in person from heaven. Then the first thing that happens is our loved ones who have fallen asleep in Christ are raised. Next, all living believers are caught up together with them. We all meet the Lord in the air. After that we shall be with Him forever. We could build a great deal upon these truths if we needed to, but we have far more than this revealed in the Bible. We could, for example, conclude that since we are forever to be with the Lord, we shall be with Him on His throne when He reigns, just as we shall be with Him when He returns to the earth. But these things are all spelled out for us elsewhere in Scripture.

What will our new bodies be like after the resurrection? The answer comes in considerable detail in 1 Corinthians 15. Notice how verse 51 ties right in with 1 Thessalonians 4. "We shall not all sleep, but we shall all be changed." Some Christians will be asleep in Christ, and will have to be raised from the dead. Others will be living at that time. In the twinkling of an eye, two things will happen. The dead will be raised in bodies that are incorruptible, that is, they will never again be subject to decay. In the same instant, those who are living will be changed. These bodies of our humiliation will suddenly be fashioned like His glorious body, "according to the working whereby he is able even to subdue all things unto himself" (Phil 3:21).

The truth in 1 Corinthians 15:35-50 is exceedingly rich. The new bodies given to all believers at that time will be like our present bodies, but only as the grain which springs from the ground is like the seed out of which it came. We will each have our own body, made as it pleases God to make it (v. 38). Now it is terrestrial, or prepared for life on the present earth. In that day it will be celestial, or prepared for life in heaven (v. 40).

By nature we lack true dignity; we possess bodies of dishonor. Someday we shall have radiantly beautiful bodies of glory (v. 43). Now we are weak; then we shall have power. Now we possess natural bodies; then we shall be given spiritual bodies. Instead of being designed as instruments of the soul, they will be designed as instruments of the spirit for life in a different environment (v. 44). Now we are earthy; then we shall be heavenly (v. 48). Now we are mortal or subject to death; then we shall be immortal or deathless (v. 53).

When Peter and John went to the sepulchre after the resurrection of Christ, they saw something so remarkable that they believed He had truly risen from the dead. The record is in John 20:4-8. As they stooped down and looked inside the tomb, they saw the linen clothes in which the body of Christ had been wrapped, still bearing the impress of the form of the Lord. The cloth which had been around His head was still coiled up, as it had been when He was buried. The body of Christ had passed through the grave clothes without disturbing them. They "saw, and believed."

This is of great interest when we read in 1 John 3:2, "when he shall appear, we shall be like him." When we put these truths alongside the records of how the Lord suddenly appeared in the closed room where the disciples were meeting (Jn 20:19), and how He moved from one place to another instantaneously, it becomes clear when we have our new bodies, we shall no longer be subject to the natural laws which now limit us.

Christians are fascinated with the question of whether we shall know each other after our present life is over. 1 Corinthians 13:12 actually provides a complete answer to this: "Then shall I know even as also I am known." However, several other passages are equally illuminating. Abraham was "gathered to his people" as though they were awaiting him (Gen 25:8). David expected to go to be with his dead son

(2 Sa 12:33). After death the rich man of Luke 16:22-24 was able to recognize the beggar Lazarus, even across the great gulf.

At the transfiguration, Peter, James, and John recognized Moses and Elijah, whom they had never met (Mt 17:1-4). Our names are written in heaven (Lk 10:20). Christ will confess us before His Father who is in heaven (Mt 10:32). The converts of Paul are to be his joy and crown of rejoicing in the presence of the Lord at His coming (1 Th 2:19).

No passage of Scripture suggests that we shall lose our capacity to recognize others. There would seem to be no point in the revelation that we shall be caught up together with our deceased loved ones when the Lord comes for us, if they are not even known to us. Nor would this passage be given as a source of comfort if we had no idea who these sleeping saints were after the resurrection.

WHAT HAPPENS AFTER THE RAPTURE

As far as we can tell by comparing Scripture with Scripture, the first thing to follow the translation of believers at the rapture is the rendering of an account for our works as Christians. "We must all appear before the judgment seat of Christ; that every one may receive the things done in his body, according to that he hath done, whether it be good or bad" (2 Co 5:10). The Greek word used here for judgment is *bema*, the raised seat or throne from which rewards were given to contestants in the ancient games of Greece. The *bema* of ancient Corinth may be seen today by tourists.

This is an individual judgment, for "every one of us shall give account of himself to God" (Ro 14:10-12). Some light upon what this means is found in 1 Corinthians 3:10-15. Fire will in some manner "try every man's work of what sort it is." All Christian service which is able to survive this trial by fire will be rewarded. If our work is burned up, we shall suffer loss of reward, but we ourselves shall be saved.

Such a revelation is given not to frighten us, but to instruct us and to teach us about our service for Christ. It is encouraging to know that our labor is not in vain in the Lord (1 Co 15:58). Alongside must be placed the warning of 2 John 8. We must look to ourselves "that we lose not those things which we have wrought, but that we receive a full reward."

The New Testament mentions five crowns to be given believers. They appear to be connected with our rewards; they can be lost by failure to "hold fast" in this life (Rev 3:11). An *incorruptible crown* awaits those who have honored the precepts of the Bible (1 Co 9:25). A *crown of rejoicing* goes to every believer who has had a part in soul winning or missionary effort (1 Th 2:19). Those who have kept the faith and loved His appearing will receive a *crown of righteousness* (2 Ti 4:8). Faithful endurance under severe trials leads to a *crown of life* (Ja 1:12). A crown of glory will be awarded to each Christian who has fed the flock of God and has been an example to the flock (1 Pe 5:2-4).

The time when believers receive their rewards is stated in Revelation 22:12, "Behold, I come quickly; and my reward is with me, to give every man according as his work shall be." Evangelicals agree this text speaks of the coming of the Lord to receive His Church, rather than His coming to the earth the second time.

One other outstanding passage has to do with Christian rewards. When the marriage of the Lamb takes place in heaven, His Bride is said to be arrayed in fine linen, clean and white. The fine linen is the righteousnesses (marg.) of the saints (Rev 19:7, 8). Students over the centuries have understood that—since the garments of the Bride are referred to as the righteousnesses, or righteous acts of saints—these acts are their works performed on earth, and rewarded at Christ's return for the Church when the *bema* judgment is held. In some manner which passes comprehension, our good works become the white garment worn by us when we are united forever to our Lord in marriage. It is impossible now for us to understand fully these wonderful truths expressed in our limited vocabulary.

What Happens After Christ's Return

After mention of the marriage of the Lamb, Revelation 19:7-9 declares, "Blessed are they which are called to the marriage supper of the Lamb." Commentators hold this is to take place in heaven, immediately following the marriage. But many are convinced the marriage supper will be held on earth after Christ returns, and that it may even be a figure for the rejoicing of the saints during the Millennium.

To support this view, they point out the parable of the ten virgins portrays an earthly scene, and that some manuscripts and versions render Matthew 25:1 as concluding with, "the bridegroom and the bride." Furthermore, the parallel passage in Luke 12:36 speaks of the lord returning from the wedding. In any case, the wedding supper awaits every believer.

After the rapture, inhabitants of earth will not again see those who were translated until "the coming of our Lord Jesus Christ with his saints" (1 Th 3:13). We shall be with our Lord when Christ descends with the armies of heaven to deliver His earthly people and vanquish His enemies at Armageddon (Rev 19:14; Zec 14:5). A tremendous change will have taken place in believers as they return in their new bodies. Christ will be "glorified in his saints . . . admired in all them that believe" (2 Th 1:10). Glorification will have wrought such a transformation in us that Christ will be praised by those who see us, because He will have changed a company of ordinary people in such a way that they reflect His own glory.

What shall we be doing after He returns with us? One revealed truth is that we shall serve Him (Rev 22:3). As He sits on the throne of His glory judging the nations, we shall sit with Him. It is written, "the saints shall judge the world . . . we shall judge angels" (1 Co 6:2, 3). We shall be closely associated with the Lord in all that He does. Doubtless, administering our inheritance (Ac 26:18) will form a part of our service, an inheritance not described except that it will be incorruptible, or beyond the reach of death, undefiled, or beyond the reach of sin. It "fadeth not away," so that time cannot touch it; it is reserved in heaven for us, so that it is beyond the reach of loss (1 Pe 1:4).

Another revelation is found in John 17:3, "This is life eternal, that they might know thee, the only true God, and Jesus Christ, whom thou hast sent."

Eternal life is knowing God. The horizons of our minds will expand forever as we learn more and more of the infinite mind of God. The fear of the Lord is only the beginning of knowledge (Pr 1:7). The human mind draws back in awe and amazement at the contemplation of what it will mean to keep growing forever in our knowledge of the mind of the God who made no two snowflakes or sunsets alike.

A third revelation concerning our eternal future is found a number of times in the New Testament. The Lord has promised that we shall sit with Him in His throne (Rev 3:21). We shall reign on the earth (Rev 5:10). If we are to understand Luke 19:17-19 literally, then we will be given authority over actual cities in the kingdom. This coming reign with Christ by believers is somehow related to present afflictions, because "if we suffer, we shall also reign with him" (2 Ti 2:12). Moreover, it is written about the saints that "they shall reign for ever and ever" (Rev 22:5), so that this will be eternal.

One of the old Puritans, speaking to a poor congregation who knew greater afflictions than most today, said, "As the angels of God move through this church this morning, they do not look upon us as a company of little known, rather poorly clad followers of Christ. They look upon us as though we were already robed in the royal purple of universal sovereignty. For the Lord has chosen us to reign with Him forever and forever, and He is now preparing us to sit with Him upon the throne of the universe!"

6

The Lord Jesus Christ in Prophecy—
The Kinsman-Redeemer

DANIEL FUCHS

> If thy brother hath become poor, and hath sold away some
> of his possession, and if any of his kin come to redeem it, then
> shall he redeem that which his brother sold.
> After he is sold he may be redeemed again; one of his
> brethren may redeem him (Lev 25:25, 48).

IN OUR STUDY of Old Testament Scriptures, we realize the Jews
were never perfect and were never expected to be perfect. Some
Bible teachers believe that because our Lord called the Jewish
people for His specific purposes, they should have been perfect.
We, too, should be perfect, but we all fall short of that goal.
Because the Jewish people were weak and imperfect, part of
the Law which was given to them was to keep them from getting into trouble; other parts of the Law were given to help
them out of trouble. One of the latter laws is the law of the
kinsman-redeemer, in Hebrew, the law of the *goel*. "One of his
brethren may redeem him" (Lev 25:48).

A Jew could get into trouble three thousand years ago in the
same way many Jews and Gentiles get into trouble in the twentieth century—by contracting debts they could not pay. However, there is this difference: there were no bankruptcy laws in

the Old Testament. In those days, if a Jewish person contracted a debt, the debt had to be paid even if it meant he had to sell himself into slavery. Under this law of the *goel*, when a Jew became a slave, in a sense he was a voluntary slave because he got into debt of his own volition. When that occurred, God had a wonderful way of escape for him. The nearest living relative, the next of kin, became the *goel*, his kinsman-redeemer; it was the privilege of the *goel* to redeem his brother from his voluntary slavery.

There was another way one might be able to pay his debt. After the Law was given at Sinai, God divided the land among the twelve tribes. Observe that the Word of God teaches clearly that God is and always was the Owner of the land. But, there is a distinction between ownership and possession, and He gave possession to Israel and to no other nation. "The land shall not be sold for ever, for the land is mine for ye are strangers and sojourners with me" (Lev 25:43).

In order to pay his debt, it frequently was necessary for the one who was the possessor of the land to sell the use of that land to another family, or perhaps a member of another tribe, or even to a member of another nation. If that happened, it became the privilege of the nearest living relative to redeem the possessions which his brother had wasted away. The word "*goel*" is also frequently used in conjunction with the Hebrew word for *the blood, "hadam";* for if a Jew was wrongfully slain, it was the duty of the nearest living relative to become the *goel hadam*, the avenger of the blood.

So the kinsman-redeemer had a threefold duty: first of all, he redeemed his brother from his voluntary slavery. Second, he redeemed the possessions which his brother had wasted away. Third, he became the avenger of the blood for his brother who was wrongfully slain. Our message is this: *The Lord Jesus Christ is our Kinsman-Redeemer.* He is eligible to be our Kinsman-Redeemer because through the incarnation He became our Kinsman!

Have you ever wondered about the miracle of the incarnation? Of all the great miracles recorded in the Scriptures, the greatest one is the death of the Lord Jesus Christ. He is the Author of life. "He is before all things and by him all things consist" (Col 1:17). How could He die? The second greatest miracle is the incarnation. How could God become a man? We cannot explain this, but we believe it. We do not know how God became man, but we do know of many reasons why He did. He had to be a Man in order to become our Kinsman-Redeemer.

In India there is a religion called Brahmanism. One of its tenets is reincarnation: when a man dies, his soul goes into the body of an animal. Therefore, a Brahman will never knowingly hurt any animal, not even an ant. A missionary was teaching a high caste Brahman about the Lord. The man was fascinated with the Gospel of the Lord Jesus Christ. But, there was an intellectual stumblingblock. He could not understand the mystery of the incarnation, how God would ever become a man.

One day as he walked in a field he pondered the missionary's message. It was a sunny day, and as his shadow crossed a huge ant hill, he noticed the tiny ants became frightened and ran helter-skelter. He did not want to frighten these creatures, and he wondered how it would be possible to tell them that he did not hate them. He came to the conclusion that the only way he could ever tell the ants that he did not hate them, would be to take upon himself the form of an ant, live among them as an ant, and speak their language.

This Brahman was a thoughtful man and so came to another conclusion. Although he had been taught to believe that God was a God of condemnation and judgment, he now concluded that God wanted to tell people that He loved them. God did what that Brahman could not do; He took upon Himself the form of sinful man. He came among man, spoke our language, and said, "God so loved the world that he gave his only begotten Son, that whosoever believeth in him should not perish, but have everlasting life" (Jn 3:16). This is what the Lord Jesus Christ did when He became our Kinsman. He became eligible to become our Kinsman-Redeemer. But He not only became our Kinsman, He also is our nearest Kinsman.

Who is your nearest relative? Is it your mother or your father? How we can thank God for godly parents! But, think about some of the young Hebrew Christians whom we meet daily. Many of them are ejected from their homes and rejected by their peers. What a blessing for them to know that the Lord Jesus Christ is the One of whom the psalmist spoke, "When my father and my mother forsake me, then the LORD will take me up" (Ps 27:10). Is your closest living relative your brother? The Lord Jesus Christ is that Friend that sticketh closer than a brother!

Because the Lord Jesus Christ is our nearest Kinsman, He is eligible to become our *goel,* our Kinsman-Redeemer. He has done that, for He has redeemed us from our slavery. One may say, "Slavery? I'm an American. I never was a slave, and I never will be a slave." Let us pray this will always be true, especially in light of happenings in our country today. However, the plain teaching of Scripture is that "all have sinned and come short of the glory of God" (Ro 3:23). Our Lord said, "Whosoever committeth sin is the servant [slave] of sin" (Jn 8:34). Here is the terrible thing about our slavery to sin: we become voluntary slaves to it. No brother of ours ever sold us into slavery as Joseph was sold into slavery by his brethren. We thought we were free and we would never become slaves; but one day we awakened to the fact we were shackled, slaves to our appetites, passions, and desires. We had become voluntary slaves to sin. But, listen to the Gospel message: "If the Son therefore shall make you free, ye shall be free indeed" (Jn 8:36).

How eloquently Charles Wesley expressed this truth that the Lord Jesus is our Kinsman-Redeemer and has redeemed us from our slavery to sin:

> He breaks the power of cancelled sin,
> He sets the prisoner free;
> His blood can make the foulest clean;
> His blood availed for me.

The Saviour also fulfilled the second office of the kinsman-redeemer. He has redeemed the possessions which we wasted away because of our sin. When a man sins, he loses the most wonderful possession that he can have, his conscious sense of fellowship with the living God. When a man sins, that fellowship is broken. "But your iniquities have separated between you and your God, and your sins have hidden his face from you, that he will not hear" (Is 59:2).

But 1 John 1:7 reads: "If we walk in the light, as he is in the light, we have fellowship one with another, and the blood of Jesus Christ His Son cleanses us from all sin."

We have a wonderful Kinsman-Redeemer, One who has redeemed us from our slavery to sin and redeemed the possession which we wasted away because of our sin. When the Lord Jesus Christ redeemed the possession which we wasted, He gave us something we never had before. Some believe that the purpose of God in redemption was to wipe the slate clean, so that we would all be in the same state Adam and Eve were in the Garden of Eden. However, experience has taught us that if God's purpose in redemption was to cleanse our sin and return us to the Garden of Eden, we would do the same thing all over again.

God has given us something that Adam and Eve never had. He has given us the hope of heaven and the promise of eternal life. Heaven is not a place where we will walk on streets of gold or sit on little thrones and strum harps throughout the ages of eternity. Nor is heaven a place of idleness. What is heaven like? All that we do know of heaven is from the Word of God and from our Kinsman-Redeemer, who, before He died to redeem us, told us about heaven. He said that heaven is a place. "I go to prepare a place for you." The wonderful thing about that place is that it has been prepared for us by the One who loves us and the One who knows exacly what we need and what we want. Also, I know that when we get to heaven we are going to be surprised: "Eye hath not seen, nor ear heard, neither hath entered into the heart of man the things which God hath prepared for them that love him" (1 Co 2:9).

Not only are we going to be surprised, we are also going to be completely satisfied. The Lord Jesus Christ, our Kinsman-Redeemer, the One who made all things, the Creator and Sustainer, is now preparing a home for us, His redeemed ones. The greatest satisfaction, however, is not in what He has prepared for us, but in the fact that we shall see Him face to face. There will be worship, adoration, praise, and instruction; and then we will have all of the ages of eternity to be satisfied in Him!

As certainly as Jesus Christ has taken upon Himself the first two offices of the Kinsman-Redeemer, we can be assured from the Word that He will take upon Himself the third of those offices. He is going to become the *goel hadam,* the avenger of the blood. In our own generation 6 million Jews were slain because of the madness of Adolf Hitler. What about the millions of martyrs? Church history of the early centuries as well as today's news from Soviet Russia and China tell of modern martyrs whose blood is being shed wantonly.

How long? How long will truth be on the scaffold, and wrong on the throne? The Word of God assures us the time will come when our Lord Jesus Christ will return, and He will be the Avenger of the blood. We will hear from heaven these words, "The kingdoms of this world are become the kingdoms of our Lord and of his Christ; and he shall reign for ever and ever" (Rev 11:15).

I started my work with the American Board of Missions to the Jews on Throop Avenue in Brooklyn, New York in 1937 as a boys' worker. It was a tough but wonderful job. It was one of those tasks you think is nothing but failure while you are doing it. Yet the Lord overruled. Five of those boys who came to the camera class I had on Throop Avenue are now either on the mission field or are pastors. I enjoyed the boys and many of them accepted the Lord. I remember one September asking them what they would like to study from the Bible. I was amazed when they told me they wanted to study the book of Revelation.

Until then I had never thoroughly studied the Revelation, but then I had to. Shortly after I began to teach Revelation, Dave, one boy who had accepted Jesus as Lord and Saviour, stopped coming to class. I could not visit Dave at home because his parents were extremely antagonistic toward us; so I timed a walk down Broadway to coincide with the closing of school. Finally, an hour later, Dave came out. I said, "Hi, Dave. Where have you been? Haven't seen you for quite a while. What's wrong?"

He answered, "Well, I'll be very frank with you. You've been studying the book of Revelation, and I'm scared of what you're teaching us from that book."

I was taken aback and replied, "Dave, you're a believer in the Lord. Is there anything in your life that is hindering your fellowship with Him?"

He looked me in the eye and said, "No, sir."

Then I told him, "Dave, you have no right to fear anything written in the Word of God. Revelation was written for comfort, and this book has been of more comfort to believers than any other book in the Bible throughout all of the ages of the Church."

"How can you get comfort from these things?" he asked.

Then I showed him that some scenes in this book were on earth, and some were scenes in heaven; and that when these terrible things were happening on earth, the believers in the Lord Jesus Christ were in heaven. I then read to Dave these words of comfort:

> These are they which came out of great tribulation, and have washed their robes and made them white in the blood of the Lamb. Therefore are they before the throne of God and he that sitteth on the throne shall dwell among them . . . and shall lead them unto living fountains of waters: and God shall wipe away all tears from their eyes (Rev 7:14-15, 17).

"Dave," I said, "are you afraid of that?"

And he answered, "No, sir."

I then said to him, "If I were Adolf Hitler, the last book in the Bible that I would ever read would be Revelation, because this book tells of the time when the Lord Jesus Christ is to take upon Himself the office of the Avenger of the blood. There will not be one drop of shed blood that will be unrequited." These were words of comfort for Dave.

Around that time a New York newspaper published a cartoon. The main object in it was a hand with the index finger pointed forward. The hand was breaking through clouds, representing the power of God. On that index finger there was a tiny figure with his arm upraised and his fist clenched. He had his hair combed to the side, and he wore a little moustache. Out of his mouth came the words, "My will is supreme." (Adolf Hitler actually said that!) The cartoon was so well drawn that one could see the thumb of God closing down on that figure. Some people say that thumb has already closed down, but Adolf Hitler is going to face the great white throne judgment; and he will not escape until he has paid every farthing.

It is not always going to be "truth forever on the scaffold, wrong forever on the throne." A day is coming when our Lord Jesus Christ will return, and the kingdoms of this world will become the Kingdom of our Lord and of His Christ. And He shall reign forever and ever.

We have a wonderful Kinsman-Redeemer, One who has redeemed us from our slavery to sin, One who has redeemed the possessions which we wasted away because of our sin, One who has given to us the hope of heaven and eternal life, and One who is to return and become King of kings and Lord of lords.

And our Kinsman-Redeemer shall reign forever and ever!

7

The Prophetic Message of the Book of Ruth

DANIEL FUCHS

NEVER JUDGE the value of a book of the Bible by its size! The book of Ruth, a literary and spiritual gem, is a small book with a great message.

> The book of Ruth occupies a unique place in Scripture. It is set between Judges and Samuel. Judges gives you failure in Israel, "every man did that which was right in his own eyes." There was no king. In Samuel you have the king anointed, crowned, and the kingdom established. The book is therefore a *parenthesis* between failure in Israel upon one side, and the glory of the kingdom upon the other (I. M. Haldeman, *Bible Expositions,* 1:60).

In the Hebrew Bible, the book is placed between the Song of Solomon and Lamentations. There are five books in the Hebrew Scriptures called "Megillot," each of which is read at different feasts or fasts which commemorate past events: The Song of Solomon at Passover; Ruth at Pentecost; Esther at Purim; Lamentations on the Ninth of Ab; Ecclesiastes at Tabernacles. As we shall see, the reading of Ruth in the synagogue at Pentecost is highly significant.

The author's purpose is made abundantly clear in the genealogy at the close of the book.

> Now these are the generations of Pharez: Pharez begat Hezron, and Hezron begat Ram, and Ram begat Amminadab, and Amminadab begat Nahshon, and Nahshon begat Salmon, and Salmon begat Boaz, and Boaz begat Obed, and Obed begat Jesse, and Jesse begat David (Ru 4:18-22).

To some casual readers of the Scriptures the genealogies of the Bible are dry and uninteresting. But these genealogies are gold mines of spiritual and prophetic truth. The more one digs in these mines the richer he becomes.

The purpose of the book of Ruth is to provide solid historical validity to the kingship of David, not just to alleviate the dismal tone of the book of Judges by inserting "a beautiful idyll of the times." In God's prophetic purpose the genealogy at the end of Ruth is quoted by Matthew as he demonstrates that the Lord Jesus Christ is heir to David's throne. A comparison of the genealogy in Ruth and in Matthew 1:3-5 shows clearly that Matthew quoted (probably from memory) the book of Ruth. Without the book of Ruth the record of the Gospel of Matthew could not be complete.

In Jewish Missions one cannot overstress the importance of the genealogies. Dr. Leopold Cohn, the rabbi who, under God, founded our ministry, vividly testifies to this fact:

> The following Monday, I called on the minister and found him a Hebrew-Christian with a most interesting, winning way. He was educated in Talmudic literature and when he told me that he was a descendant of a certain well-known rabbi, he gained my confidence and love at once. Seeing my utter ignorance of the Christian faith, but also my great earnestness, he gave me a Hebrew New Testament, asking me to read it. I opened it at once and read for the first time in my life: "This is a book of the generation of Yeshua, the Messiah, the son of David, the son of Abraham." My feelings could not be described!

For many years my thoughts had been occupied almost continually with the coming of the Messiah. For that reason I had suffered and left my wife and children for a strange country, which I never expected to visit. I had inquired of several rabbis, searched the Scriptures, prayed and thought; my whole being was wrapped up in this one subject. And now at last here was a book that would tell me about the Messiah. "Surely," I thought, "this book has come to me directly from above. God has sent it to me, and it will give all the desired information and lead me to the Messiah." The words, "Yeshua, the Messiah, the Son of David, the Son of Abraham" were sweeter to me than angelic music. I forgot all about my troubles and became very happy, and running as fast as I could to my private room, the doors of which I locked behind me, sat down to study that book. I began reading at eleven o'clock in the morning, and continued until one o'clock after midnight. I could not understand the contents of the whole book, but I could at least realize that the Messiah's name was Yeshua, that He was born in Bethlehem, that He had lived in Jerusalem and talked to my people, and that He came just about the time indicated by the angel's message to Daniel. My joy was unbounded (Leopold Cohn, *To An Ancient People*, pp. 21-22).

We now begin to see the importance of the book of Ruth, and the more we read it the more we realize that both the Old Testament and the New Testament are one Book—the Word of God.

As we study the purpose of the book of Ruth we must understand one principle which shows unity throughout the Scriptures, namely, that the central theme of the Scriptures is Christ. At the dawn of human history with the first sin, God gave the first promise of the Redeemer from sin,

> And I will put enmity between thee and the woman, and between thy seed and her seed; it shall bruise thy head, and thou shalt bruise his heel (Gen 3:15).

The Redeemer was to be the seed of the woman. There would be a struggle between Him and Satan; He would suffer but would be victorious. It is possible that Eve thought that Cain was the promised Messiah for when he was born she exclaimed, "I have gotten a man, the Lord" (Gen 4:1, Luther's translation). Later prophecies limited the Seed to come from the line of Abraham, and even later from the tribe of Judah. The Messiah had to come from Adam, Abraham, and Judah (and, even later, through David). This explains the reasons why we have the genealogies, and it also clearly shows the importance of those laws of Israel which are so prominent in the book of Ruth: the law of the kinsman-redeemer, and the law of the Levirate marriage.

> Yet we should miss the whole spirit of the narrative, if, while admitting the influence of other matters, we were not to recognise that the law of redemption and of marriage with a childless widow, for the purpose of "not putting out a name in Israel," had been the guiding principle in the conduct of all these three — Naomi, Ruth, and Boaz. And, indeed, of the value and importance of this law there cannot be fuller proof than that furnished by this story itself — bearing in mind that from this next-of-kin union descended David, and, "according to the flesh," the Lord Jesus Christ, the Son of David. (Alfred Edersheim, *Bible History*, 1:186-87).

Three-hundred-fifty years before, God had made provision for Ruth. In the Law, He had made provision for the kinsman-redeemer. "After that he is sold he may be redeemed again; one of his brethren may redeem him" (Lev 25:48).

Three-hundred-fifty years later, Ruth met her kinsman-redeemer, Boaz, who was a kinsman of Naomi. It was the duty of the near kinsman to take the wife of the deceased and raise children in *his* name. However, in Ruth's case, there was a living, eligible relative closer than Boaz, who had first choice. He was willing to redeem the possession but not the person! When told that he would have to marry Ruth, he demurred saying, "I cannot redeem it for myself, lest I mar mine own inheritance: redeem thou my right to thyself; for I cannot redeem it" (Ru 4:6).

Boaz was both eligible and willing. He redeemed the property and Ruth, and she became his wife. He publicly advocated her before the elders and inhabitants of the city. In this, Boaz is a perfect type of the Lord Jesus Christ. Our Lord became our Kinsman through the incarnation, when He took on human nature. One of the purposes of the incarnation was to fulfill the requirement—"One of his brethren may redeem him" (Lev 25:48).

Our Lord became our Redeemer by virtue of His death: "And they sung a new song, saying, Thou art worthy to take the book, and to open the seals thereof: for thou wast slain, and hast redeemed us to God by thy blood out of every kindred, and tongue, and people, and nation (Rev 5:9).

At this point we must be careful in our exegesis. Some will say that since Boaz is a type of the Redeemer and Ruth was his bride, that Ruth is a type of the Church. Then they will continue that since Ruth was a Moabitess, a Gentile, she is a type of the Gentile Church. The Scriptures do not teach a Gentile Church. "For he is our peace who hath made both one and hath broken down the middle wall of partition between us" (Eph 2:14).

Ruth does not represent the Church. She is a beautiful illustration of the believer who chooses the God of Israel to be her God.

Provision under the Law was made for Ruth, not only for her redemption but also for her sustenance. The twenty-third chapter of Leviticus is one of the great prophetic chapters in the Old Testament. A famous rabbi, Samson Raphael Hirsch, once wrote, "The catechism of the Jew consists of his calendar." This twenty-third chapter is a synopsis of Israel's sacred calendar. Verses 4 through 44 list the "holy convocations" of our Lord.

As we carefully study this list, we can observe at least three significant facts. First, all of these convocations are mentioned frequently in both the Old Testament and the New, and they all have prophetic significance. Second, the New Testament clearly teaches that some of these feasts have already been fulfilled by the Lord Jesus Christ. Third, some of these have not yet been fulfilled.

Summarizing briefly, in Leviticus 23:4-21, we have a synopsis of the fulfilled feasts: Passover (vv. 4-5); Unleavened Bread (vv. 6-8); Sheaf of First Fruits (vv. 9-14); Pentecost (vv. 15-21). Verses 23-44 are a synopsis of the unfulfilled convocations: The Feast of Trumpets (vv. 23-25); Day of Atonement (vv. 26-32); Feast of Tabernacles (vv. 33-44).

Between the fulfilled feasts and those still to come, there is a verse that at first seems to be out of place; this verse made the book of Ruth possible.

> And when ye reap the harvest of your land, thou shalt not make clean riddance of the corners of thy field when thou reapest, neither shalt thou gather any gleaning of thy harvest: thou shalt leave them unto the poor, and to the stranger. I am the Lord your God (Lev 23:22).

As one reads this verse and the book of Ruth, he realizes that 350 years before Ruth, God made provision for her sustenance, just as before the foundation of the world He made provision for her redemption.

Ruth said, "Let me now go to the field, and glean ears of corn after him in whose sight I shall find grace." When Boaz saw Ruth gleaning he commanded his young men to leave "handfuls on purpose for her" (Ru 2:16). In studying the prophetic significance of the book, we realize we are gleaning in fields where "handfuls on purpose" have been left.

Between the spring feasts of Israel's calendar, all of which have been fulfilled by our Lord, and the convocations of the fall, four long months elapse. Between Pentecost and the future Feast of Trumpets, millions like Ruth have gleaned in Boaz's field. The author of the book of Ruth had to explain the mystery of how a Moabitess could become an ancestress of King David. The New Testament explains a greater mystery that is taking place in this dispensation.

> For this cause I Paul, the prisoner of Jesus Christ for you Gentiles, if ye have heard of the dispensation of the grace of God which is given me toward you, how that by revelation he made known unto me the mystery: (as I wrote afore in a few words, Whereby, when ye read, ye may understand my knowledge in the mystery of Christ) which in other ages was not made known unto the sons of men, as it is now revealed unto his holy apostles and prophets by the Spirit: that the Gentiles should be fellow heirs, and of the same body, and partakers of his promise in Christ by the gospel (Eph 3:1-6).

"That the Gentiles should be fellow heirs." Earlier I indicated that reading the book of Ruth in the synagogue at Pentecost was significant. Each year for two thousand years Israel has been reminded that one who had been an accursed Moabitess became the ancestress of David. Now again during this present age provision has been made for the poor and the stranger. These are just gleanings; the harvest is not yet.

Once there was famine in the land of Judah. It was in the Lord's land and among the Lord's people. The judges ruled, and each man did what was right in his own eyes. Because of the famine the family of Elimelech departed from the land, but instead of life they found death. Naomi heard that the Lord had "visited his people in giving them bread" (Ru 1:6), and she longed to return to the land. What a sad picture of Israel in dispersion—widowed and desolate.

The prophet Amos foretold a time when there shall be a great famine, not of bread but "of hearing the words of the Lord" (Amos 8:11). But the long summer of Israel's dispersion and silence comes to a close soon.

Once more Israel is a nation, and many like Naomi have returned, still in unbelief. The time of the judges when men please themselves shall cease. The trumpet will soon sound, and we long for it. "Behold, I show you a mystery: we shall not all sleep but we all shall be changed in a moment, in the twinkling of an eye at the last trump" (1 Co 15:51-52).

The time of the judges is closing. The King is coming! This is the prophetic message of the book of Ruth.

8

Egypt's Place in God's Program

WENDELL G. JOHNSTON

THE APRIL 9, 1973 edition of *Newsweek* had a significant article on Egypt that is interesting to Bible students:

> Few world leaders can match Egypt's President Anwar Sadat for verbal overkill. Back in 1971, he declared that the "year of decision" was at hand, and when he failed to meet a succession of self-imposed deadlines for recapturing Israeli-occupied territory, he simply flipped a page of the calendar and marked 1972 as the year for "inevitable" battle. Nothing ever came of these threats, and for a while it seemed that Sadat had lost his taste for predicting the impossible. But last week, the Egyptian leader was rattling his sabers again—and this time he vowed that he meant exactly what he said. In a speech to the Egyptian People's Assembly, he proclaimed an "era of total confrontation" with Israel (p. 43).

Egypt is very much in the news today, particularly as it pertains to the nation Israel and the Middle East. As you are well aware, Egypt is very much in the Word of God. The Bible has much to say concerning Israel and many nations. In Ezekiel, Isaiah, and Jeremiah there are twenty-five chapters that pertain to the nations. Apparently, God has a message that He wants to convey to us through these nations: the way He deals with them, how they respond to Him or refuse to respond. Little time is spent in study of the Old Testament prophecies that pertain to the nations.

In the minor prophets, God has much to say about other nations. Amos tells about the judgment that is coming on Damascus; he mentions the judgment that is coming to the Philistines, Tyre, Ammon, and Moab. You can just see the people as they listen to these prophecies and to these messages from Amos.

They are actually applauding what he is saying, and probably some are saying, "Pour it on, Amos, say some more," because the people of Israel want to see the judgment of God upon these other nations. However, when he finishes with the nations, he moves to Judah and Israel, and warns them of God's judgment that is coming as well as God's blessing. All through the Old Testament, interwoven with the story of Israel is the story of nations, and very prominent in this is the nation of Egypt.

Throughout the Old Testament, God warned His people about their relationship with Egypt. With the exception of the time when Joseph and Mary were fleeing because of the danger to the life of Jesus, there was really no reason for Israel to go to Egypt. The people of Egypt were godless and unconcerned about Jehovah. God's people were never sent there, but many of them disobeyed and went. So it was that Israel's contact or alliance with Egypt represented disobedience. God rescued His people from a time of bondage and suffering, making Egypt the instrument to demonstrate His great power.

There is significant prophecy in the Old Testament concerning Egypt's downfall in three major portions of Scripture— Isaiah 19, Ezekiel 29—32, and Jeremiah 46. In Isaiah 19 the prophecy concerning the downfall of Egypt has already been fulfilled, through verse 15. Beginning with verse 16, Isaiah set forth a then future course of the nation, which we can see now in modern history. In this chapter the religion of the people in Egypt is described:

> And the spirit of Egypt shall fail in the midst thereof, and I will destroy the counsel thereof: and they shall seek to the idols, and to the charmers, and to them that have familiar spirits, and to wizards. And the Egyptians will I give over into the hand of a cruel lord; and a fierce king shall rule over them, saith the Lord, the Lord of hosts (19:3-4).

If you have ever been in Egypt you will understand the spiritual condition there. God promised judgments against the nation which were to teach the Egyptians about Himself. In Ezekiel 29:6 we read: "And all the inhabitants of Egypt shall know that I am the LORD, because they have been a staff of reed to the house of Israel." Verse 16 of that chapter reads in part: "But they shall know that I am the Lord GOD." In 30:8 the prophet declared: "And they shall know that I am the LORD, when I have set a fire in Egypt, and when all her helpers shall be destroyed." And then 30:19: "Thus will I execute judgments in Egypt: and they shall know that I am the LORD." Ezekiel 30:26 states: "And I will scatter the Egyptians among the nations and disperse them among the countries; and they shall know that I am the LORD." Egypt's problem is that of other nations and of the world today: they are unconcerned about God. The prophecy of Isaiah 19 is that their religious system will fail, and in the future the Egyptians will learn about the true God.

A downfall of the government of Egypt is prophesied in Isaiah 19:2: "And I will set the Egyptians against the Egyptians, and they shall fight everyone against his brother, everyone against his neighbor; city against city, and kingdom against kingdom"—a civil war within the nation. Even today one can see that there is mistrust among them. One man is set against another. There seems to be so much hatred there.

Ezekiel 29 also speaks of this:

> And I will make the land of Egypt desolate in the midst of the countries that are desolate, and her cities among the cities that are laid waste shall be desolate forty years: and I will scatter the Egyptians among the nations, and will disperse them

through the countries. Yet, thus saith the Lord GOD; at the end of forty years will I gather the Egyptians from the people whither they were scattered: and I will bring again the captivity of Egypt, and will cause them to return into the land of Pathros, into the land of their habitation; and they shall be there a base kingdom. It shall be the basest of the kingdoms; neither shall it exalt itself any more above the nations: for I will diminish them, that they shall no more rule over the nations. And it shall be no more the confidence of the house of Israel, which bringeth their iniquity to remembrance, when they shall look after them: but they shall know that I am the Lord GOD (vv. 12-16).

The Scripture says that Egypt will be a very insignificant nation, one of the least, a very base kingdom. We have witnessed in history this certainly has been true of Egypt. All they have is their past glory. When my wife and I visited there several years ago, that is all they had to show—the ancient glories. This is a prophecy given by Isaiah and Ezekiel which has been fulfilled, although we shall see a different role for Egypt in the last days.

Economic decay is prophesied in Isaiah:

And the waters shall fail from the sea, and the river shall be wasted and dried up. And they shall turn the rivers far away; and the brooks of defense shall be emptied and dried up: the reeds and the flags shall wither. The paper reeds by the brooks, by the mouth of the brooks, and every thing sown by the brooks shall wither, be driven away, and be no more. The fishers also shall mourn, and all they that cast angle into the brooks shall lament, and they that spread nets upon the waters shall languish. Moreover they that work in fine flax, and they that weave networks, shall be confounded. And they shall be broken in the purposes thereof, all that make sluices and ponds for fish (19:5-10).

This speaks of a time of want, when there will be a great need;

and certainly this has been fulfilled, because it has been true in Egypt for many, many years.

Intellectual decay is also mentioned in Isaiah:

> Surely the princes of Zoan are fools, the counsel of the wise counsellors of Pharaoh is become brutish: how say ye unto Pharaoh, I am the son of the wise, the son of ancient kings? Where are they? where are the wise men? and let them tell thee now, and let them know what the LORD of hosts has purposed upon Egypt. The princes of Zoan are become fools, the princes of Memphis are deceived, they have also seduced Egypt, even they that are the stay of the tribes thereof. The LORD hath mingled a perverse spirit in the midst thereof: and they have caused Egypt to err in every work thereof, as a drunken man staggereth in his vomit. Neither shall there be any work for Egypt, which the head or the tail, branch or rush, may do (19:11-15).

As you read through Isaiah 19, you notice the prophet speaks of the decay of Egypt. This land which was once a great power, beginning with the government itself, became insignificant. There will be no help religiously for the people of Egypt. Economic decay, intellectual decay—what a sad picture for Egypt. This is true; Scripture has been fulfilled to the very letter. The philosophy of Egypt was the philosophy of Satan. In Isaiah 14, as the prophet begins to unfold the prophecies concerning the nations, he brings out very clearly that behind the actions, the thoughts, the programs of the nations, is really the domination of Satan himself. Satan's philosophy and spirit brought Egypt's downfall.

What is Egypt's future in God's prophetic picture? Daniel 11:1-35 is a historical narrative; you see the major events in the Persian Empire. When you come to verse 36, there is a change, and the movement is away from the historical; it goes to the future. This was often the way the prophets spoke. Sometimes they would speak about events that were in their day, and then suddenly they would speak of the future. The reason for this is that a prophet would prophesy things which would take place immediately, so that these could be tested to prove he was a prophet who could be trusted for the future. The test of a prophet was, Is his prophecy fulfilled? So Daniel spoke about something that had taken place. Then he moves to that which will be future.

> And the king shall do according to his will; and he shall exalt himself, and magnify himself above every god, and shall speak marvellous things against the God of gods, and shall purpose till the indignation be accomplished: for that that is determined shall be done (Dan 11:36).

The king of whom he is talking is the king mentioned in Daniel 2, 7 and in Revelation 13, 17. This is the man of sin, the one who will come out of the Western confederacy, an alliance of nations. He will claim to be God and will have great power on the earth. He will endeavor to change laws, and he will blaspheme God. This is to be in the time of tribulation which is future for us today. The attitude of this king is expressed by the prophet: "Neither shall he regard the gods of his fathers, nor the desire of women, nor regard any god: for he shall magnify himself above all" (Dan. 11:37).

The king of the South, or Egypt, is mentioned in verse 40. In the historical record in Daniel 11:1-35, notice references to the king of the South, or to Egypt. Verse 5 has a reference to the king of the South; also in verses 9, 11, 14, and 25 (twice). From a study of history, it can be verified that the references relate to the leaders, the rulers of Egypt. In verse 40, projecting to the future, during the time when the Antichrist, the man of sin, will be ruling, Daniel says:

> And at the time of the end shall the king of the south push at him: and the king of the north shall come against him like a whirlwind, with chariots, and with horsemen, and with many ships; and he shall enter into the countries, and shall overflow

and pass over. He shall enter also into the glorious land, and many countries shall be overthrown: but these shall escape out of his hand, even Edom, and Moab, and the chief of the children of Ammon. He shall stretch forth his hand also upon the countries: and the land of Egypt shall not escape (11:40-42).

Apparently, in the last days, during the time of tribulation, the seven-year period known as the time of Jacob's trouble, Egypt again is going to gather strength and be an important nation; and Egypt and those around her will go into battle against the man of sin and be defeated.

Isaiah gives us the final message concerning Egypt, predicting God's blessing upon that nation:

> In that day shall there be an altar to the LORD in the midst of the land of Egypt, and a pillar at the border thereof to the LORD. And it shall be for a sign and for a witness unto the LORD of hosts in the land of Egypt: for they shall cry unto the LORD because of the oppressors, and he shall send them a savior, and a great one, and he shall deliver them. And the LORD shall be known to Egypt, and the Egyptians shall know the LORD in that day, and shall do sacrifice and oblation; yea, they shall vow a vow unto the Lord, and perform it. And the LORD shall smite Egypt; he shall smite and heal it: and they shall return even to the LORD, and he shall be intreated of them, and shall heal them. In that day shall there be a highway out of Egypt to Assyria, and the Assyrian shall come into Egypt, and the Egyptians into Assyria, and the Egyptians shall serve with the Assyrians. In that day shall Israel be the third with Egypt and with Assyria, even a blessing in the midst of the land: whom the LORD of hosts shall bless, saying, Blessed be Egypt my people, and Assyria the work of my hands, and Israel mine inheritance (19:19-25).

It is interesting to me that as we look at the future of the nation Egypt, we see that it will become more powerful, even as we are witnessing in our day. Since 1922, the Egyptians have been able to rule themselves, although they have had British soldiers there, because the British wanted to protect their Suez interests. In 1946, the soldiers were removed. Today Egypt grows in power and significance. Abdul Nasser's rise brought Egypt to prominence. In his attempts "to drive Israel into the sea," he built new strength into Egypt.

His successor, Sadat, has taken a course which has been more conservative but with seemingly greater long-term gains. In July, 1972, Sadat made a historic decision when he asked the Russian technicians to leave his borders. He is pointing the way to a strong and independent nation more amenable to peaceful coexistence with Israel for the present. During the Tribulation, Egypt will battle against the man of sin and be defeated, according to Scripture. Wonderful blessing is finally predicted for the Egyptians. God will bless them only on one basis, that they fall on their knees before Jehovah God and recognize Him.

The words of the apostle Paul seem most fitting here, "O the depth of the riches both of the wisdom and knowledge of God! how unsearchable are his judgments, and his ways past finding out!" (Ro 11:33).

Only a God of mercy could open His heart to a sinful people. God's dealings with Egypt are just an illustration of His great love for all the world.

9

The Career of a Roughrider on the Tough, Ten-Horned Beast

Clarence E. Mason, Jr.

Revelation 17 presents a dramatic vision with some obvious emphases, but clothed in certain symbols that we must be very careful to interpret. Some have posed real problems for earnest Bible students. Note verse one: "And there came one of the seven angels who had the seven bowls of wrath, and talked with me, saying unto me, Come hither; I will show you the judgment of the great harlot that sits upon many waters."

Almost immediately, verse 15 identifies what these waters mean: "The waters which you saw, where the harlot sits, are peoples, and multitudes, and nations, and tongues."

This identification emphasizes an important point. Bible symbols are always interpreted *in the Bible,* either in the immediate context (as here) or somewhere else (e.g., Is 60:5).

The harlot is said to be the one "With whom the kings of the earth have committed fornication" (v. 2). Throughout the Old Testament, idolatry is pictured as adultery (e.g., Jer 3:6-9). Israel, symbolically, is represented as married to Jehovah. To take the love and worship due to God alone (her Husband), and to prostitute it on idols is like a wife giving herself to another man. Verse 3 continues: "So he carried me away in the spirit into the wilderness."

There he sees a beautifully clothed woman, bejewelled and spectacular, but with such amazing accompaniments as "full of the names of blasphemy . . . and in her hand a golden cup full of abominations and filthiness of her fornication" (vv. 3-4). She is seen seated on "a scarlet colored beast, having seven heads and ten horns," and on her forehead there is a name written: "MYSTERY BABYLON [omitting the comma] THE GREAT, THE MOTHER OF HARLOTS AND ABOMINA-TIONS OF THE EARTH . . . drunken with the blood of the saints, and with the blood of the martyrs of Jesus: and when I saw her, I [was astounded]. And the angel said unto me, [Why are you astounded]? I will tell [you the secret concerning the woman and concerning the seven-headed, ten-horned beast that carries her on its back]" (vv. 5-7).

Our first reaction is, "What a strange, unusual woman, in a strange unlikely place, mounted on such a weird beast! What could it possibly represent?" Who would expect to see such a gorgeously apparelled woman *in a wilderness?* The whole thing is intriguing.

There are two *major* identifications necessary. First, who or what is the beast? Second, who or what is the woman? There are a number of secondary and corollary, but important, adjuncts to these two questions: How do you interpret "Babylon"? What is the identity of "the seven mountains"? And, what are "the seven heads, and the eighth"? This evil city is seemingly connected with both the woman and the beast, and not with just one of them. What view is correct? And then, there is verse 8 about the beast that "was" and "is not" and "ascends out of a bottomless pit" and then "goes into perdition."

But, first of all, look at the beast, "having seven heads and ten horns" (vv. 3, 9, 12). Fortunately, by the time we arrive at this part of the Bible, there is no reason to guess; there has been abundant opportunity to identify. Let us trace some of the evidence. In chapter 7 of Daniel, we find four empires, beginning with Babylon, as in chapter 2. The image of chapter 2 and the beasts of chapter 7 are parallel and trace the history of the times of the Gentiles from then until Jesus Christ comes back the second time to set up His 1,000-year Kingdom.

In chapter 2, the head of gold is Babylon in the person of its king, Nebuchadnezzar II; the chest and two arms appropriately picture Medo-Persia; the belly and thighs represent Greece; and the legs, feet, and toes symbolize Rome. Correspondingly, in chapter 7, the winged lion, prominent on Babylon's great gates, was a widely known current symbol of Babylon; the bear, Medo-Persia; the leopard, Greece; and the nondescript, composite beast is Rome. Light is thrown on the fourth beast by Revelation 13:2, where we read of the final form of the fourth beast with ten horns (Dan 7:7): "And the beast I saw was like a leopard (i.e. Greece), and his feet were as the feet of a bear (Medo-Persia), and his mouth as the mouth of a lion (Babylon), and the dragon gave him his power, and his throne, and great authority."

Thus, the fourth beast is seen as composed of three previous kingdoms. Indeed, this was the genius of these great kingdoms. They helped themselves to the military and political expertise of the previous kingdoms and only discarded what was of no value. Proof of this viewpoint is found in chapter 2, when the stone (the Lord Jesus) smites the image, He does so on its final form (feet/toes); *but* the image is viewed as intact and still standing. Thus Gentile world power is pictured as a continuing force with Nebuchadnezzar until the final, ten-toed (ten-horned) form of the revived fourth Western (Roman) empire is smashed by our Lord at His return to earth.

The beast on which the harlot sits is undeniably the revived form of the fourth empire. The Revelation 13 chapter division interrupts the thought at the end of Revelation 12. Revelation 13:1 should be read after 12:17 without a break. Further, the "I" should be *he*. We should read: "And the dragon was wroth with the woman, and went to make war with the remnant of her seed, which keep the commandments of God, and have the testimony of Jesus Christ. And he [the dragon] stood upon the sand of sea, and [I] saw a beast rise up out of the sea, having seven heads and ten horns."

The ultimate, ten-divisioned form is pictured as though the dragon (Satan) calls it forth from the sea of nations. So in chapter 17 we deal with the same person, or group, or system brought before us in Daniel 7 and Revelation 13. The beast is both the historically oriented fourth empire, which seems to have gone out of existence, and the final form of that empire which, to the amazement of the world, will be reconstituted ("the deadly wound . . . healed," Rev 13:3). And the dragon, who in the end-time accomplishes this, is, according to Revelation 12:9, Satan.

The near and far view are also apparent in the case of the woman of chapter 12, as well as the beast. Originally the woman gives birth to the man child (plainly the Lord Jesus) who will rule with a rod of iron. Satan, using the then Roman Empire through Herod (the beast), sought to destroy Him at Bethlehem. But He was spared. But the woman, Israel, is later viciously persecuted by the dragon through the beast in the seventieth week of tribulation, according to the remainder of chapter 12. Thus, the continuing factor of the woman and that of the beast and the dragon show that God omits the whole Church age and kaleidoscopes the *whole* career of Israel (the woman), the beast (Rome), and the dragon (Satan). It was Israel, not the Church, that gave birth to Christ.

So, whether it be chapter 12, or 13, or 17 of Revelation, the beast is the fourth empire. Satan (the dragon) gets the worship he has so long eagerly sought, as we read: "And they worshipped the dragon that gave authority to the beast" (Rev 13:4). Satan is indeed "the prince of this world, the god of this world."

He mounted a rebellion against God with his challenge, "I

will be like the Most High" (Is 14:14). He sought to divert the praise of the angelic host from God to himself. For this, he was cast out of heaven as an abiding place. This nefarious person is the driving force behind the nations generally, but particularly in relation to fanning Gentile hate for Israel, reaching a climax in the end of the times of the Gentiles. Since he cannot vent his hate on God, he perennially seeks to harm God's people. He will horribly maul Israel: "And it was given to him to make war with the saints *and to overcome them* (Rev 13:7).

Satan is set free to act at his nefarious worst through his henchmen, to a degree never before permitted.

However, we want to examine the relationship of the revived fourth empire with the woman of Revelation 17, rather than with Israel, the woman of Revelation 12. Note verse 9: "The seven heads are seven mountains on which the woman sits, and there are seven kings."

Various interpretations have been given, but I suggest the seven heads equate with seven mountains. As we have seen from Daniel 2, and many other Old Testament passages, mountains carry the symbolic thought of rule or authority. The stone that smites the image of Daniel 2 becomes a great mountain, filling the whole earth. This is tacitly said to be the universal rule or Kingdom of our Lord Jesus Christ, culminating in His return to destroy Gentile world power and supersede it with His own. I would suggest, therefore, that "seven kings" do not mean seven actual men, but rather should be understood to mean seven spheres or kinds of rule.

Observe, by John's time five of the seven have fallen and "one is" (v. 10). The imperial form of government, instituted by Julius Caesar, was present in John's day. Thus, the chronological sequence of political Rome was as follows: (1) kings; (2) consuls; (3) dictators; (4) decimvirs (an oligarchy of "ten men"; (5) military tribunes; and (6) emperors.

The first five had fallen by John's day; the sixth, the imperial, "is." And "one is yet to come." This seventh form is the revived form of rule, because the imperial form, then present in John's day, ceased in the West in A.D. 476, and in A.D. 1453 in the East, when its last bastion, Constantinople, fell to the Saracens.

I think it is plain that the seventh form of Roman government is "yet to come." That form of Rome has not yet been established, though there are harbingers.

What evidence is there that the revival of the Western (fourth) empire is on the way? The Common Market has done much to bring Europe back together. Six nations signed a treaty on historic Capitoline Hill in Rome fourteen years ago. They were Belgium, France, Italy, Luxembourg, the Netherlands, and West Germany. For a number of years attempts were made to expand the Market. On January 1, 1973, a great event took place; the *six* became *nine!*

God has some very important things to say about "the ten" who will *eventually* constitute the revived fourth Western empire. Evidently this is getting the world ready for this ultimate ten. The revived empire must reach as far east as the Euphrates. But the framework and drive for reunification of the West are there. Listen to these significant quotations from the Common Market magazine, *The European Community:* "January 1, 1973 marks the most important event in the European Community's fourteen year history; important, too, for its future."

It goes on to say: "What will this mean for the future?"

And the statement concludes: "Change is *the only certainty.*"

Now, watch *their* evaluation of the increased merger: "Many observers see in the addition of Britain and Denmark, with their strong democratic traditions, the strengthening of the European Parliament."

We quote further:

> Many Danes and Britains have already spoken out in favor of the Vedel Report, which calls for a *directly elected* European

parliament with real powers in the Community's decision-making process. This "European union" may not be the United States of Europe of which the Community's founding fathers dreamed, but it amounts to *much more* than an enormous trade bloc.

These words are weighted with overtones of biblical terms. It goes on, next, to say: "Since the small countries have traditionally supported a united rather than a national approach to international problems, their new influence *can only accelerate Europe's political union*" (italics mine).

The Bible states that the West will be united politically in due time. It has been gathering momentum since World War II. First, there was the formation of Benelux (Belgium, Netherlands, Luxembourg) in 1944, followed by Western European Union (1948), NATO (North Atlantic Treaty Organization) in 1949. Next came the European Coal and Steel Community (1954) and more recently the Common Market (1959). I understand the Western hegemony will include all that *was* Rome before its fall, but also all that came out of Rome, namely, North and South America, which were colonized by Western Europe.

Perhaps we should deal with those strange words of verse 8. Many have professed to see a sinister raising from the dead of Judas, Nero, or some other nefarious person. I believe the similar words of verse 11 are significant and the best explanation of verse 8. It is not an individual of the past, but the *Roman Empire* which, as explained above, went out of existence historically, but will be revived by Satanic power.

This trend is without parallel. Historians are amazed that the Western empire's "deadly wound" is being healed. The "seventh" head or king(dom) is the ultimate ten-divisioned "United States of the Western World." Some superstatesman will be held in such high regard by the ten, that they will cooperate by delegating their power to him (vv. 13, 17). There is no indication that *men* will recognize any satanic activity in the reestablishment of the Western hegemony. It will be attributed, no doubt, to the skill and charisma of this superleader.

This Western power (Rev 13:1-10), with Rome as headquarters, will make a treaty with Israel, permitting restoration of blood sacrifice. But the Jewish leader in Jerusalem (Rev 13:11-18) will betray the faithful in Israel and, in the midst of the week, he will break the treaty with them by causing blood sacrifice to cease through desecration of the sanctuary. He does this by placing an *image* of the Roman political leader in the holy place (Mt 24:15; Rev 13:12-15; Dan 9:27). He precipitates the last three and a half years of Daniel's seventieth week, called the Great Tribulation by our Lord (Mt 24:21; cf. vv. 15-24). Thus, the seventh head or king(dom) moves into a new, hellish form of power—"the eighth" (Rev 17:10-14), which is the same man and same kingdom, but now fully seen to be dominated by Satan (Rev 17:11; 13:1-10; 13:11-18; 12:11-17). His particular target is God's repentant remnant Israel, who refuse his attempts to break their spirit when they refuse to blaspheme God by worshipping the image of the Roman beast as commanded by the apostate Jewish ruler, ally of the man in Rome (Rev 13:11-18).

It is significant that, to prepare the way for Rome to be capital of the West, prophecy is being fulfilled as evidenced by the growth of that city. It has grown from 214,000 in 1871, to 1,700,000 in 1936, and now to 3,000,000, despite ten years effort by city fathers to slow down this surge to Rome from all over Italy. Certainly a capital city should be outstanding ("the great city," Rev 17:18), and it is!

So much, then, for the tough, ten-horned beast! Now, let us observe the harlot woman, the roughrider on the beast. She is identified by the term *Babylon*. Among earlier premillennialists, it seems that there was almost unanimity in equating this Babylon of Revelation 17-18 with the thesis that ancient Babylon would be rebuilt on the Euphrates. They professed to see Revelation's Babylon as the origin and source of false doctrine

and idolatry at Babel in Genesis 11. They followed this with
the reminder that Babylon was the capital of the first of the
four empires of the times of the Gentiles. However, they cou-
ple these obvious facts with the gratuitous assumption that
Babylon is the literal name of a literal city to be rebuilt on the
Euphrates in the end time.

I do not believe this view can be sustained. There are two
reasons why: first, there is a striking analogy of the use of ancient historical names for another city. Revelation 11:8 points
out the fate of the two witnesses: "Their dead bodies shall lie in
the street of the great city, which is spiritually called Sodom
and Egypt, where our Lord was crucified."

Notice the word *Jerusalem* is not used, although Jerusalem
is meant, for that is where Christ was crucified. In other words,
the *spiritual* characteristics of "Sodom" and "Egypt" will characterize Jerusalem in the end time. Likewise, Rome, the city
of the seven hills in history and prophecy, will have the *spiritual* characteristics of that ancient great, pagan city, Babylon,
out of which came all false doctrine, starting with Nimrod and
the tower of Babel. It is out of "the mother of harlots" that
false doctrine has come. Thus, the ultimate confusion and col-
lision of false doctrine will take place in Rome in the end time.

In the second place, to hold the theory of a future rebuilt
Babylon on the Euphrates does violence to valid interpretation
of fulfilled prophecy. Read Isaiah 13:19-22: "But Babylon,
the glory of the kingdoms, the beauty of the Chaldeans [e.g.
Nebuchadnezzar's ziggurat and world-famous hanging gar-
dens], shall be as when God overthrew Sodom and Gomorrah.
It shall never be inhabited, neither shall it be dwelt in from
generation to generation . . . but wild beasts of the desert shall
lie there . . . her time is near and her days shall not be prolonged."

Similar prophecies are given in Jeremiah 50:40 and 51:
60-64. With these words before us, I submit that if the nearby
little village of Hillah is to be considered as continuing Baby-

lon, valid prophetic fulfillment has lost its meaning. If over-thrown, multicenturied, deserted Babylon is not a fulfillment, what *is* fulfillment? Babylon has, according to normal prophetic fulfillment, been utterly destroyed.

Now, let us look at the woman herself and see how political union (the ten-horned beast) and religious union (the woman) relate to each other, closely associated as chapter 17 makes them. Since the Reformation, the woman has been interpreted as the Roman Catholic church. We can understand the Reformers' preoccupation with the Roman church, but I believe the tendency to call everything to do with Rome anti-Christ is an oversimplification and has led to many mistakes of interpretation. There are elements of truth here, but a distortion of truth.

Now, I do not deny the Roman church had part in past error or will have in the future pictured by the woman. But it is a great mistake to limit the woman to the Roman church. For instance, per contra, to follow the analogy of the woman as the church and the beast as the political power, far from the woman riding the beast, in a real sense during the first three centuries, the beast "rode" the woman, when the Church was being bitterly persecuted by imperial Rome!

Further, the woman was relatively pure then, whereas in Revelation 17 she is pictured as filthy. Indeed, it is a typical misconception, fostered by the Roman church, that she began with Christ and the apostles. The fact is that the *old* Catholic preceded the *Roman* Catholic church by five centuries.

But with Constantine's marrying of the political power (beast) with the religious power (woman), we do have a union which has persisted since then. But remember; not only did the *Roman* church use its power, conniving with the political power to dominate people and even governments, but also the great state churches of Protestantism have done so.

Do not forget that our Mayflower forefathers fled England to escape religious persecution by the Church of England, nor that Luther gave his blessing to the butchering of the Anabaptists in Europe. Do not forget also the terrible slaughter of Jews in the name of the church as well as the state. As late as Hitler, where was any real protest in Europe to Jewish slaughter from the established Protestant churches?

So I feel that the ultimate form of the woman (as well as the historic church) will be a conglomerate of false religion, pictured by a false bride of Christ, over whose destruction all heaven will one day rejoice (Rev 19:1-10). Jesus will not destroy her; He leaves that to the unclean beast with whom she has so long sinned! Certainly, the ultimate woman of this chapter will be heavily flavored by the Roman church, but constituted of apostate Protestantism as well! I believe also that the cults, and perhaps the occult, will be involved. As a result of the demythologizing of the pope by Vatican I and II, when the true Church is translated to heaven, there will be a speedy union of everything professing Christ in the Western world, or perhaps everything "religious."

The seeds of ecumenism are blossoming rapidly, and this monstrosity, still posing as the bride of Christ, will prevail upon the political power to accede to her desires. Already today in Washington, in the capitals of the world, and through the World Council of Churches, lobbies are at work to pressure the political powers. Coming events cast their shadows before, and we can already see the shape of things to come as they affect the woman and the beast.

So the religious power (woman) will ride the political power (beast). But the hatred, the resentment, the frustration of the centuries on the part of political leaders will finally reach its climax in the man in Rome and his associates. Though the beast is tough, so is the woman. But one day, as they go for a ride, the word will be fulfilled: "God has put it in their hearts to fulfill his will" (v. 17).

They will trample her; they will devour her. Everything of her system that can be used, they will use. But she is a tough one. Some things about her cannot be eaten and "digested."

So the bones and remainder will be "burned" and obliterated. The beast cannot brook even the memory of her, hating her with such a consuming hatred! Thus, this is the ultimate end of the career of the harlot roughrider on the tough ten-horned beast.

I understand the overthrow of the harlot by the political leader of the West will take place when he feels strong enough to do so, namely, at the middle of Daniel's seventieth week. The setting up of the image of the Roman political beast by his Jewish associate in the Jerusalem Temple, thus desecrating it, will be the dramatic signal for this complete change in the religion of the West. The desecration will cause sacrifice to cease (indeed, will stop all worship in the Western world) and precipitate that awesome last three and a half years which our Lord called the *Great* Tribulation. Thus all religion will be centralized to honor the man who "exalts himself above all that is called God or that is worshipped." (Compare 2 Th 2:4 with Mt 24:15; Rev 13:14-15; Dan 9:27.)

God would have us foresee, and those living then properly interpret, these two crucial movements or systems that climax here. The *city* is not simply the site of the Vatican, but will be the capital of religion. It will also be the political capital of the Western entente in the days ahead of us. The Western reunion which started at Paris, shifted to Brussels, will some day be set up—not in London or New York or Paris—but in Rome. That city is geographically, historically, and prophetically the inevitable capital of the Western world. No wonder it has seen amazing growth in recent years.

To summarize: the beast is both a *man* heading the revived West (Rev 13:1-10; 17:11-15) *and a system*, the hegemony of ten combined nations (17:12, 15-17). It is indissolubly anchored in the ancient seven hilled *city* of Rome (17:5, 18). The woman is a *system*, a conglomerate of false religion (17:1-7, 16) and is also inextricably linked with the *city* of Rome (17:18).

She, at first, dominates the beast. But, probably in the middle of Daniel's seventieth week she will be overthrown by the beast (the political power) who supersedes to the religious power as well. Later the city and the fourth (revived) empire will also fall, and its two leaders will be hurled alive into perdition, the lake of fire (Rev 19:20).

10

Principles Governing National Destiny

S. MAXWELL CODER

THE NATIONS OF THE WORLD are mentioned at least 760 times
in Scripture. In the Old Testament the Hebrew word *goy* occurs 600 times. In the New Testament the Greek word is
ethnos, found 160 times. The importance of this subject is
somewhat obscured by the fact that four different English words
are used to translate these Hebrew and Greek words. They are:
nations, Gentiles, heathen, and people. Usually the text refers
to nations as we know them today. Sometimes individuals are
in view, as in Acts 11:1, "the Gentiles had also received the
word of God." Gentiles in such passages are persons who did
not descend from Abraham through Jacob, as did the Jews.

The nations are a neglected theme of divine revelation. Ser-
mon material prior to the present century contains very little
on the subject. Bible dictionaries and encyclopedias offer no
significant help. A technical work on prophecy published as
late as 1958 contains a bibliography of 958 books and titles
devoted to prophecy; but lists only one short article on the nations, a brief study of Daniel 2.

We are now living in the times of the Gentiles or nations
(Lk 21:24). These times began when God brought to an end

the national sovereignty of Israel and gave world government into the hands of the Gentiles (Dan 2:38). Cyrus was able to say, "The LORD God of heaven hath given me all the kingdoms of the earth" (Ezra 1:2). The times of the Gentiles are said to be fulfilled when they no longer control Jerusalem (Lk 21:24); their actual end is generally understood to be described in Daniel 2:44, when the Kingdom of God replaces all other kingdoms.

When that end comes, the world as we have known it will be drastically changed. Instead of being divided into many nations with the people of Israel scattered among them, it will be one world governed by the Lord as King over all the earth (Zec 14:9), and the Jews will be regathered in their ancient land as the leading nation. Some nations will continue to exist under the sovereign control of the Lord; others will vanish from the earth.

Throughout history many nations have been born, have come to great power and wealth, only to grow weak and die. Historians have sought to explain why the great empires of antiquity perished. The study of Gibbon's *Decline and Fall of the Roman Empire* and similar works brings to light an interesting list of possible reasons for the decay and fall of Rome. They include bureaucratic corruption, the power and cost of the military, heavy taxation, the dole, inflation, debasing of the currency, decline of cities, moral degeneracy with the decline of the family, the spread of Eastern religions, and the growth of astrology and divination.

As the 200th anniversary of the United States approaches, serious questions are raised as to whether the presence of many of these same evils may not point to the imminent end of America. Doubtless, there is validity in the question, but the only true answer is found in the Word of God, where principles are revealed by which the destiny of any nation may be determined. Five of these may be said to be prominent in the Bible.

RELATIONSHIP TO GOD

"Blessed is the nation whose God is the LORD" (Ps 33:12). When a Christian from India saw for the first time the rich farms and cities of America he commented, "It is my earnest conviction that the difference between my own impoverished country and this one is to be found in the fact that the United States has sought to honor the true God." National blessing is experienced by any country which puts its trust in God; judgment comes upon those which do not. "The nation and kingdom that will not serve thee shall perish; yea, those nations shall be utterly wasted" (Is 60:12).

The Old Testament contains the records of the destruction of many nations which defied the God of Israel, or which were given over to idolatry and the worship of false gods. The name of Egypt is on that dreadful roll. There are the records of godless Assyria, Tyre, and the land of the Philistines (Zep 2:5). It is written, "The wicked shall be turned into hell, and all nations that forget God" (Ps 9:17). After the Lord's return all nations or Gentiles will be gathered before Him, and the announcement of the psalmist will be fulfilled as some hear the words, "Depart from me, ye cursed, into everlasting fire" (Mt 25:32, 41). There are nations today which must inevitably come under this doom from God, and perish because of their godlessness.

RELATIONSHIP TO THE LAW OF GOD

"Righteousness exalteth a nation: but sin is a reproach to any people" (Pr 14:34). This principle is to be distinguished from the first. Israel is an example of a nation whose God was the Lord, but which perished because of disobedience to the law of God. Untold blessings were promised Israel "if thou shalt hearken diligently to the voice of the LORD thy God," but the curse of God would result from failure "to keep his commandments and his statutes which he commanded thee" (Deu 28:1, 45).

There is a point beyond which God will not permit a nation to go in sin. The Amorites who inhabited Canaan were a wicked people, but in Abraham's day the longsuffering of God was seen in His words, "the iniquity of the Amorites is not yet full" (Gen 15:16). He knew their sin would reach the point where they would have to be destroyed, but that day had not yet come. It came when Joshua led the Israelites into Canaan and overthrew the seven nations of that land (Ac 13:19). The terrible statement appears in Leviticus 18:25 that the land vomited out her inhabitants because of their sin.

Sodom and Gomorrah were overthrown because their sin was "very grievous" (Gen 18:20; 19:24, 25). At the time of the return of Christ, the days of Lot will again be seen on earth (Lk 17:28-30). It is startling to read in Ezekiel 16:49 that in addition to the abominations of Sodom, her iniquity was "pride, fulness of bread, and abundance of idleness," words which sound like a description of the days in which we live.

Relationship to Satan and the Unseen World

Satan is described in the Scriptures as a being who weakens the nations and shakes kingdoms (Is 14:12, 16). He deceives the whole world (Rev 12:9). In Old Testament days he stood up against the nation Israel (1 Ch 21:1). He now controls the kingdoms of the world; he offered them to Christ (Mt 4:8, 9). His angels were active behind the scenes in ancient Persia and Greece (Dan 10:13, 20). In the dark days of the Great Tribulation three unclean spirits will come out of the mouth of the dragon, Satan, and "go forth unto the kings of the earth and of the whole world, to gather them to the battle of that great day of God Almighty" (Rev 16:13, 14).

One reason given for the destruction of the nations of Canaan by the Lord was that they used divination, observed times, used enchantments, witchcraft and consulted familiar spirits (Deu 18:9-14). Comment is hardly necessary concerning present times, in view of the floodtide of these same satanic practices today. Every newspaper carries its column on astrology; book stores carry countless books on the occult; spiritism and witchcraft seek contact with the world of demons; and satanism flourishes. These practices can lead only to judgment on the nation which is deceived by them.

RELATIONSHIP TO THE PRESENT PROGRAM OF GOD

It has always been God's purpose to have His way of salvation made known among all nations (Ps 67:2). He is now visiting the Gentiles to take out of them a people for His name (Ac 15:14). To accomplish this purpose He leads His people to proclaim the Gospel everywhere. He is longsuffering, not willing that any should perish. "The longsuffering of our Lord is salvation" (2 Pe 3:9, 15).

This is one of the keys of history. Why has not the Lord intervened to ring the curtain down on human history when there has been great cruelty or injustice among nations? Because He is seeking many sons for glory. He wants to save men from perishing. Nineveh was saved from destruction because of the preaching of Jonah. England was saved from the effects of the French Revolution because of the preaching of the Wesleys. A favorable response to the message of God can deliver any nation from divine judgment.

It is also historically true that nations which further the evangelizing of the lost, as does the United States, for example, know the favor and blessing of God, while those which oppose the gospel experience His judgment. The great commission calls for the teaching of all nations. It will be fulfilled. People from every kindred, tongue, people, and nation will be in glory (Rev 5:9), and those nations which help in the fulfillment of the great commission are more likely to continue into eternity than those which do not.

RELATIONSHIP TO THE PEOPLE OF ISRAEL

The best known of all these Bible principles is first stated in

Genesis 12:3, "I will bless them that bless thee, and curse him that curseth thee." God at the first allocated land to the nations on the basis of the number of His people Israel (Deu 32:8), and He has said that anyone who touches Israel touches the apple of His eye (Zec 2:8). Because the nation of Edom mistreated the Jews, it was desolated by divine judgment (Num 20:21; Ez 25:12-14). Jeremiah wrote about Israel, "first the king of Assyria hath devoured him; and last this Nebuchadrezzar king of Babylon hath broken his bones. Therefore thus saith the Lord of hosts, the God of Israel; Behold, I will punish the king of Babylon and his land, as I have punished the king of Assyria" (Jer 50:17, 18).

The decline of Spain began after it expelled all its Jews in 1492, the same year the Lord opened a new door for them in the New World. During World War II an older believer who knew the Word said, when the overthrow of the British Isles seemed almost certain, "God will not permit England to be overthrown, because she has been a place of refuge for the Jews, and a source of great missionary activity. I am convinced that Hitler's Germany will be destroyed instead, for daring to touch the apple of God's eye." He was right, of course.

God promised to bless Israel's friends and curse her enemies. Remarkably, when the nations are judged, after the return of Christ, on the basis of the way they have treated His brethren, the people of Israel, He uses these same words. The friendly Gentiles are called "ye blessed of my Father." All others are told, "Depart from me, ye cursed, into everlasting fire" (Mt 25:34, 41).

THE DESTINY OF AMERICA

In the light of these five divinely revealed principles, it is an interesting exercise to consider the destiny of America and other living nations. Will the United States survive and continue into the new earth, or will it perish? Does the Bible have anything to say about its future, apart from the final issue of whether it will be able to endure the coming judgment of the throne of Christ's glory? Surprisingly, the Scriptures have a great deal to say about what is going to befall the nations before that judgment takes place, and a sufficient revelation to satisfy every believer concerning the destiny of his own country.

As far as America is concerned, every student knows it is not mentioned in the Bible. A number of attempts have been made to identify it under some other name, with a signal lack of success in the judgment of most conservative Christians. Here is a new approach to this subject.

There are at least sixty references in the Word of God, to all nations at the time of the end, together with a number of passages which speak of all mankind. It goes without saying that if America still exists as a nation in the end times, these passages of Scripture apply to it, as well as to every other nation. Here are seven revealed facts drawn from this body of truth.

1. America will lose all of its Christians when the Church is translated to be with the Lord forever (1 Th 4:16, 17). This will be accompanied by the removal of the restraining power of the Holy Spirit, who dwells in the Church. The lawlessness predicted in Matthew 24:12 will spread over this country.

2. Prayers for those in authority, offered by Christians everywhere, will no longer ascend to the throne of grace (1 Th 2:1, 2). Distress and perplexity will then overtake the nation (Lk 21:25), to the point of madness (Jer 25:15, 16).

3. As the Gospel of the Kingdom is preached in all the world, announcing that the Kingdom is at hand (Mk 1:14, 15; Mt 24:14), a great multitude will turn to the Lord from every nation, including America (Rev 7:9, 14). This means a great spiritual awakening.

4. Among the earthshaking events of the Great Tribulation, war, famine, pestilence, and earthquake will decimate the population of all countries, not excluding our own. The wrath of God, of the devil, and of wicked men will even threaten the existence of the human race (Mt 24:22).

5. The language of Revelation 13:1-8 seems to require that the United States will be governed by a world dictator. During his rule demonic powers will gather America and all other nations against Jerusalem, where they will suffer defeat at the hands of the returning King of kings and Lord of lords (Zec 14:1-5).

6. Christ will come in His glory and judge the nations, then establish His Kingdom over all the earth (Mt 25:31-46). The righteous will be invited to enter the Kingdom; the unrighteous will be cast into everlasting fire.

7. When the heavenly Jerusalem comes down from God out of heaven, shining in the light of the glory of God, we read that "the nations of them which are saved shall walk in the light of it: and the kings of the earth do bring their glory and honor into it" (Rev 21:10, 23, 24). This means that nations will exist in eternity.

WILL AMERICA SURVIVE OR PERISH?

As we apply the principles determining national destiny to this divinely given revelation about the future of all nations, we can certainly hope, with good reason, that the United States will continue to exist. There is widespread rejection of God today; lawlessness is increasing everywhere; satanism and occult practices are rising. Over against these evils are the continuing prayers of millions of believers that God may be pleased to send a national awakening before the tribulation dawns.

In favor of the continuing existence of the nation we love are the undeniable facts that America has always been a haven for God's ancient people Israel. He has wonderfully kept His promise to bless those who bless the children of Abraham. We may well believe He will bless America by preserving it until the coming of His Kingdom, in spite of its present sins.

There is also general agreement that the United States is still the greatest source of missionaries, prayers for missions, and financial support for God's work everywhere in the world, as it

has been for several generations. We know that when judgment finally comes, God will not destroy the righteous with the
wicked (Gen 18:23). All believers will be taken away in the
rapture before "the days of Lot" return again to the earth; and,
doubtless, there will afterward be many who like Lot will survive the coming conflagration.

As "the days of Noah" come again to mankind, we may
hope that many will survive the Tribulation period to inhabit
the earth after it is cleansed for the coming Kingdom. We have
good reason for thinking America may be among the nations
which will enjoy eternity in the presence of the Lord.

11

God's Judgment of the Nations

DANIEL FUCHS

GOD'S JUDGMENT of the nations is a biblical theme where one studies prophecy by studying history. If Old Testament history were a drama, the *dramatis personae* would be God, the nations, and Israel. After mankind failed and was judged at the tower of Babel, there was not only a division by tongues, there was also a division of the nations by families. "These are the sons of Shem, after their families, after their tongues, in their lands, after their nations" (Gen 10:31).

Old Testament history is the story of Israel's relation to God on one hand, and her relation to the nations on the other. It was never God's purpose that Israel should monopolize the truth of God. God called Abraham from Ur of the Chaldees as the instrument to channel God's blessings to the nations. "And I will bless them that bless thee, and curse him that curseth thee: and in thee shall all families of the earth be blessed" (Gen 12:3).

As we study Old Testament history we realize its philosophy is basically that the Jews are in the hands of the nations, but these nations themselves are in the hands of God. The nations perish; Israel persists. Israel is judged by her relation to God; the nations are judged by their relation to Israel.

In the past nations have been judged by the Abrahamic covenant. God blessed those nations that blessed Abraham and cursed those that persecuted him. As we seek to illustrate this truth we must clarify our position. We believe that there are many prophecies in the Old Testament which have already been fulfilled; however, in the study of prophecy we are futurists, not historicists. We believe that the vast majority of the prophecies, including those of the Abrahamic covenant, have not yet been fulfilled. We also realize that many of the prophecies, especially those against the nations that persecuted Israel, have been fulfilled.

> Fulfilled prophecy is a proof of inspiration because the Scripture predictions of future events were uttered so long before the events took place that no mere human sagacity or foresight could have anticipated them, and these predictions are so detailed, minute, and specific as to exclude the possibility that they were simply fortunate guesses. Hundreds of predictions concerning Israel, the land of Canaan, Babylon, Assyria, Egypt, and numerous personages—so ancient, so singular, so seemingly improbable, as well as so detailed and definite that no mortal could have anticipated them—have been fulfilled by the elements and by men who were ignorant of them, or who utterly disbelieved them, or who struggled with frantic desperation to avoid their fulfillment. It is certain, therefore, that the Scriptures which contain them are inspired (*New Scofield Reference Bible*, fn., p. 1339).

From Abraham to Christ the nations are mentioned in the Scriptures only as they relate to Israel. The enmity of the nations to Israel and thus against God in the past has invariably brought the judgment of God upon them. The nations that were judged include Egypt, Babylon, Moab, Damascus, Tyre, Ammon, Edom, and Elam.

There are two other observations to notice. God frequently used the instrument which the oppressor forged for use against Israel as His weapon of judgment against the oppressor. Pharaoh tried to force Israel into the sea, but he and his hordes were the ones who drowned. Haman built the gallows to hang Mordecai, and he perished on it himself. God also used persecution as a means of blessing. If it were not for slavery in Egypt, there would never have been a Passover. Most of the prophecies concerning the Lord Jesus Christ came at times of world or national crises. In the midst of persecution, trial, and suffering, the God of Abraham is still in control.

GOD JUDGES THE NATIONS BY THEIR TREATMENT OF THE JEWS

In the past, God judged the nations on the basis of the Abrahamic covenant. He still judges the nations for their treatment of the Jews. The maps of the world are changing. Empires of a generation ago are now fourth-rate powers. It is easy to point a finger at Turkey, Britain, France, Spain, or Germany; but we wonder if our own beloved country is now being judged, because in 1957 we insisted that Israel must withdraw from the Sinai Peninsula.

However, we know that God is now preparing the nations of the world for judgment. Ezekiel uses a very graphic sentence, "I will put hooks in thy jaws." This sentence is used in chapter 29:4 referring to Egypt and in 38:4 referring to Russia. These words seem to have been literally fulfilled in the past decade. For centuries, czarist Russia fought for a warm-water port and failed. In 1967 Soviet Russia succeeded, and now the Russian fleet sails the Mediterranean.

It is evident from Ezekiel 29 that the "hooks in the jaws" of Egypt and Russia refer to the Nile River and its source.

> Son of man, set thy face against Pharaoh king of Egypt, and prophesy against him, and against all Egypt: speak, and say, Thus saith the Lord GOD; Behold, I am against thee, Pharaoh king of Egypt, the great dragon that lieth in the midst of his rivers, which hath said, My river is mine own, and I have made it for myself. But I will put hooks in thy jaws, and I will cause

the fish of thy rivers to stick unto thy scales, and I will bring thee up out of the midst of thy rivers, and all the fish of thy rivers shall stick unto thy scales (Eze 29:2-4).

"My river is mine own, and I have made it for myself." The Nile has always been the source of Egypt's wealth. Every summer the river flows from its source in the African mountains 4,000 miles away. Each year the flood waters brought over 100,000,000 tons of rich volcanic soil to the Nile valley and made it the greatest agricultural wonderland in history.

This source of wealth was not enough for Egypt. Twenty years ago Abdel Nasser planned the huge Aswan Dam to control the waters of the Nile. The plan for this dam was the keystone of Nasser's diplomatic duplicities. He played the United States, Britain, and France against each other. Then he baited the hook that brought Russia into the Mediterranean by offering the building of the dam to Russia.

Now it appears that Russian scientists did not take into account the fact that the ecology of Russia and Egypt are not the same! Claire Sterling in an article in *The Jerusalem Post Weekly* described what is happening:

> Built without sluices, the dam is retaining all of the Nile's silt in the man-made Lake Nasser behind it. The clear water coming through the turbines is scouring the riverbed, undermining dams and bridges, and eroding the Delta coastline. It lacks the organic matter and natural fertilisers that made the Nile Valley the richest farmland on earth.
>
> New irrigation canals are spreading the endemic bilharzia disease, a debilitating intestinal and urinary infection. Worst of all, Lake Nasser is losing twice as much as had been expected in evaporation and underground seepage. . . . Now there will never be another flood in Egypt. The flood water runs into Lake Nasser and there the sediment sinks. Six hundred miles downstream the water flows so clear that you may stand on a balcony of the Hotel Semiramis in Cairo and see through the river's sandy bottom. Any Egyptian clutching at

your arm to show you this, will unfailingly add: "Terrifying, isn't it?" (Claire Sterling, "Aswan High Dam May Prove a Disaster," *The Jerusalem Post Weekly*, March 2, 1971, p. 12). Read the Scriptures, then read the newspapers. God still judges the nations on the basis of the Abrahamic covenant.

Finally, the Abrahamic covenant will be the basis for God's judgment of the nations in the future. Our Lord said,

When the Son of man shall come in his glory, and all the holy angels with him, then shall he sit upon the throne of his glory: and before him shall be gathered all nations: and he shall separate them one from another, as a shepherd divideth his sheep from the goats: and he shall set the sheep on his right hand, but the goats on the left. Then shall the King say unto them on his right hand, Come, ye blessed of my Father, inherit the kingdom prepared for you from the foundation of the world: for I was an hungred, and ye gave me meat: I was thirsty, and ye gave me drink: I was a stranger, and ye took me in: naked, and ye clothed me: I was sick, and ye visited me: I was in prison, and ye came unto me. Then shall the righteous answer him, saying, Lord, when saw we thee an hungred, and fed thee? or thirsty, and gave thee drink? When saw we thee a stranger, and took thee in? or naked, and clothed thee? Or when saw we thee sick, or in prison, and came unto thee? And the King shall answer and say unto them, Verily I say unto you, Inasmuch as ye have done it unto one of the least of these my brethren, ye have done it unto me. Then shall he say also unto them on the left hand, Depart from me, ye cursed, into everlasting fire, prepared for the devil and his angels: For I was an hungred, and ye gave me no meat: I was thirsty, and ye gave me no drink: I was a stranger, and ye took me not in: naked, and ye clothed me not: sick, and in prison, and ye visited me not. Then shall they also answer him, saying, Lord, when saw we thee an hungred, or athirst, or a stranger, or naked, or sick, or in prison, and did not minister unto thee? Then shall he answer them, saying, Verily I say unto you, Inasmuch as ye did it not to one of the least of these, ye did it not to me (Mt 25:31-45).

Please observe:

1. The time "when the Son of man shall come in his glory"—at the second coming of our Lord after the tribulation.

2. The subjects of the judgment—"all nations."

3. Three classes mentioned: sheep, goats, and brethren. The sheep are saved Gentiles, the goats unsaved Gentiles, and the brethren are the people of Israel.

4. The basis of the judgment—the treatment of "my brethren."

Observe also the words our Lord chose for this occasion and relate them to Genesis 12:3:

"Come ye blessed"—"I will bless them that bless thee."

"Depart ye cursed"—"I will curse him that curseth thee."

These words are the deliberate choice of our Lord, not an accident of language. God will bless the nations that bless Israel; God will curse the nations that curse Israel. God's future judgment of the nations will be on the basis of the Abrahamic covenant.

12

The Glory of the Lord's Return

Wendell G. Johnston

Behold, the day of the LORD cometh, and thy spoil shall be divided in the midst of thee. For I will gather all nations against Jerusalem to battle; and the city shall be taken, and the houses rifled, and the women ravished; and half of the city shall go forth into captivity, and the residue of the people shall not be cut off from the city. Then shall the LORD go forth, and fight against those nations, as when he fought in the day of battle. And his feet shall stand in that day upon the mount of Olives, which is before Jerusalem on the east, and the mount of Olives shall cleave in the midst thereof toward the east and toward the west, and there shall be a very great valley; and half of the mountain shall remove toward the north, and half of it toward the south. And ye shall flee to the valley of the mountains; for the valley of the mountains shall reach unto Azal: yea, ye shall flee, like as ye fled from before the earthquake in the days of Uzziah king of Judah: and the LORD my God shall come, and all the saints with thee. And it shall come to pass in that day, that the light shall not be clear, nor dark: But it shall be one day which shall be known to the LORD, not day, nor night: but it shall come to pass, that at evening time it shall be light. And it shall be in that day, that

living waters shall go out from Jerusalem; half of them toward
the former sea, and half of them toward the hinder sea: in
summer and in winter shall it be. And the LORD shall be king
over all the earth: in that day shall there be one LORD, and his
name one (Zec 14:1-9).

The glory of the Lord was revealed at various times during
Christ's earthly ministry. When He was born at Bethlehem,
Simeon was permitted to see something of that glory. When
he held that babe in his arms, realizing this was God's Messiah,
he said, "Now lettest thou thy servant depart in peace . . . for
mine eyes have seen thy salvation . . . a light to lighten the
Gentiles, and the glory of thy people Israel" (Lk 2:29-30, 32).
The Lord began His earthly ministry, we are told in John 2,
when He turned water into wine in Cana: "This beginning of
miracles did Jesus in Cana of Galilee, and manifested forth His
glory; and His disciples believed on Him" (Jn 2:11). At the
close of His earthly ministry (John 18:6) the soldiers came
for Him, and when they asked for Him, Jesus identified Himself.
Immediately they fell backward. It appears that at that moment the glory of the Lord was revealed in such a way that
they could not stand in His presence.

In John 12, as the Lord anticipated going to the cross, He
said, "The hour is come, that the Son of man should be glorified" (v. 23). You will find that every attribute of God was
demonstrated in Jesus Christ on the cross. The glory of the
Lord, the glory of our great God, was seen on the cross. These
were only glimpses of His glory.

When the Lord Jesus Christ returns the second time and His
feet touch the Mount of Olives—when He returns to establish
His kingdom—His glory is going to be seen as never before.
It will not be a temporary glimpse; it will be constantly visible,
and the world shall see it. The purpose of prophecy is to exalt
Jesus Christ and glorify Him. It is not to know the events to
come so we can revel in that, but it is to do something in our
own hearts. It is meant to draw us close to Him, to help us to

worship Him, and to bring us to our knees to honor and glorify Him. Revelation 19 states that prophecy is to glorify our Lord. It sets Him forth more than anything else.

The glory of the Lord's return will be considered in three different ways. First, the glory of the Lord's return *prophesied.* The prophetic word speaks of the glory of His return on the basis of what will be accomplished when He comes back to establish His kingdom. That advent is described as a restitution. Peter, in his message in Acts 3, mentions it and calls it the restitution of all things. In his prophetic message he declared that Christ is coming back again, and there will be the restitution of all things.

He will come back as the mighty warrior, the conquering One. This is revealed in Revelation 19; when the Lord returns triumphantly, He will fight against the enemies of God, against Israel's enemies. Zechariah states: "Then shall the LORD go forth and fight against those nations, as when he fought in the day of battle" (14:3). The restitution will be a devastating event, because the Lord is going to put down sin, wickedness, and the enemies of God.

When you turn to the book of Joshua, you have an illustration of how the Lord fought for the people of Israel. In Joshua 10 the children of Israel fought against a coalition of kings and their armies and slew many. Then God sent great hailstones down from heaven and killed a multitude. The Lord won a great victory that day because the Scripture states, "The LORD . . . fought for Israel" (v. 42). Now, that is the kind of devastating attack that will occur when the Lord Jesus returns to establish His Kingdom.

It will also be a time of refreshment and rest. Zechariah declares: "And it shall come to pass in that day, that the light shall not be clear, nor dark" (14:6). The bright ones, the luminaries, will not be shining; they will be congealed. It will not be like daylight nor like night; it will be altogether different because Christ is going to be the light.

There will be living waters in the land, according to Zechariah. This time of rest and refreshment is mentioned also in Isaiah 11, described beautifully by the prophet. It will be a time of reconciliation, not only among the nations, but also in the animal kingdom.

> The wolf shall dwell with the lamb, and the leopard shall lie down with the kid; and the calf and the young lion and the fatling together; and a little child shall lead them. And the cow and the bear shall feed; their young ones shall lie down together: and the lion shall eat straw like the ox. And the sucking child shall play on hole of the asp, and the weaned child shall put his hand on the cocatrice' den. They shall not hurt nor destroy in all my holy mountain: for the earth shall be full of the knowledge of the LORD, as the waters cover the sea. And in that day there shall be a root of Jesse, which shall stand for an ensign of the people; to it shall the Gentiles seek: and his rest shall be glorious (Is 11:6-10).

Rest and refreshment will come when Jesus Christ returns. This is something the politicians have promised us, but they have not been able to deliver. When Jesus Christ returns, He will deliver it.

The third thing that will happen when the Lord returns is that He will reign as King: "And the LORD shall be king over all the earth" (Zec 14:9). The ministry of the Lord Jesus is as a Prophet, Priest, and King. His prophetic ministry was seen when He was on this earth, as He taught. We enjoy His priestly ministry now; He is at the right hand of the Father, interceding for us. His kingly ministry has not yet taken place. He came as a King. When He stood trial before Pilate, He said, "For this cause came I into the world" (Jn 18:37). But His Kingdom was not of this earth, and He was rejected by the people of Israel. When He comes back He will reign as King. There must be a Kingdom, because Jesus Christ has not been glorified on the earth as He should. A number of things have been fulfilled concerning Jesus Christ, but He has not been glorified as

King. Revelation 19 reveals He comes as King of kings and Lord of lords, and all will come to worship Him. The glory of the Lord has been prophesied, and it will be accomplished when He returns.

The second major point is the glory of the Lord's return *pictured*. This is found in the New Testament, and it may be called the glory of the Lord's return dramatized. Matthew 16 is the background for the event of chapter 17. It was then Christ revealed to His disciples that He was going to Jerusalem, would die, and would be raised again. They were in Caesarea Philippi when Peter said, "Thou are the Christ [the Messiah], the Son of the living God," that is, the living one (Mt. 16:16). In contrast to gods of men's imagination who had been worshiped at this place, Jesus Christ was the living and true God. What a tremendous confession! Now, following this, in Matthew 16 Christ said, "Verily I say unto you, There be some standing here, which shall not taste of death, till they see the Son of man coming in his kingdom" (v. 28).

There really should be no break between chapters 16 and 17. "And after six days Jesus taketh Peter, James, and John his brother, and bringeth them up into an high mountain apart, and was transfigured before them: and his face did shine as the sun, and his raiment was white as the light" (Mt 17:1-2). On this occasion, as the disciples were confused now concerning the Lord's statement that He would die, after Peter had just confessed that He was the Messiah, the Lord allowed three of them to gaze upon His glory. Jesus was transfigured, and that word means that something came from within. His true nature and character, what He really was, was allowed to shine forth, so that it affected even the outer garments.

Those three men looked upon the glory of the Lord, the glory that will be revealed when He returns. It was for them a dramatizing of the Lord's second coming. For there were Elijah and Moses, Elijah to represent the saints that would be translated, Moses to represent those who had died and been raised. The central figure was the Lord Jesus Christ in His glory. Peter, James, and John on the earth represented the believing remnant looking for the coming of the Lord Jesus. Those men never forgot that experience. John tells us in his gospel, "We beheld his glory, the glory of the only begotten of the Father, full of grace and truth" (1:14). He said in his first epistle, "We have seen with our eyes . . . our hands have handled, of the Word of life" (1:1). Peter, in 2 Peter 1, spoke of the power and glory of the Lord's coming and mentioned that event, the transfiguration. He said, "We were eyewitnesses of his majesty . . . when we were with him in the holy mount" (vv. 16, 18). The glory of the Lord was pictured for Peter, James, and John.

There is a third major point concerning the glory of the Lord: the glory of the Lord's return *perceived by creation.* Perhaps most significant of all is the creation's recognition of Christ's glory. When Christ came the first time, creation recognized His coming. Over the manger was a star; it seemed to guard the manger because the Son of God was there. The angels sang from heaven, "Glory to God in the highest." At His birth the heavens recognized He was the Son of God.

At His baptism the heavens opened and God spoke. What a tremendous event it was as He began His earthly ministry, and God from heaven said, "This is my beloved Son, in whom I am well pleased" (Mt 3:17).

While He ministered on this earth, He could take the elements of water and at His command they were changed into wine; nature always responded to Him.

On the Sea of Galilee Jesus said, "Peace, be still," and the wind was calm (Mk 4:39). On another occasion He walked on the water. Nature was at His command. He was and is the Master of heaven and earth. There was never a question about it. There was only a question about it among the people. John said, "He came unto his own" (His own things). The land always responded to Him; creation responded to Him, but "his own (ones) received him not" (Jn 1:11).

When He entered into Jerusalem on Palm Sunday, He was riding on a colt. No man had ever ridden on that colt before, but He was not thrown off. He was the God of all nature, and He was the Ruler of the animal kingdom. That unbroken animal responded to Him. As He came into the city, the Pharisees, hearing the praise, said to Him, "Master, rebuke thy disciples." Jesus said, "If these should hold their peace, the stones would immediately cry out" (Lk 19:40).

When He hung on the cross, the heavens darkened, the earth quaked, because the God of nature was there, the God of all creation. The earth could not remain the same when the Creator hung between heaven and earth; nature responded.

At His ascension He was carried up in a cloud. All during His earthly ministry creation responded to Him. At His return creation will once again respond to Him. Matthew states:

> For as the lightning cometh out of the east, and shineth even unto the west, so shall also the coming of the Son of man be. For wheresoever the carcase is, there will the eagles be gathered together. Immediately after the tribulation of those days shall the sun be darkened, and the moon shall not give her light, and the stars shall fall from heaven, and the powers of the heavens shall be shaken: and then shall appear the sign of the Son of man in heaven: and then shall all the tribes of the earth mourn, and they shall see the Son of man coming in the clouds of heaven with power and great glory (24:27-30).

When Jesus Christ returns, again creation will respond. When Christ comes back to the face of the earth, every eye shall see Him. What a terrifying event for those who are without the Saviour. But what a magnificent event for those who believe He is the Messiah, the Saviour of the world, the King of kings, and Lord of lords. Zechariah 14:4 says that when He comes back and His feet touch the Mount of Olives, it will cleave in two. One part will be removed from the other, one to the north and one to the south, creating a valley so that people who are in Jerusalem can flee through this valley. Earth cannot remain the same in the presence of the Lord Jesus. Joel reveals:

> And it shall come to pass in that day [speaking of the return of Christ], that the mountains shall drop down new wine, and the hills shall flow with milk, and all the rivers of Judah shall flow with waters, and a fountain shall come forth out of the house of the Lord, and shall water the valley of Shittim (3:18).

Isaiah 35:1 adds: "The desert shall blossom like a rose." In Psalm 97 the psalmist says:

> The LORD reigneth; let the earth rejoice; let the multitude of isles be glad thereof. Clouds and darkness are round about him: righteousness and judgment are the habitation of his throne. A fire goeth before him, and burneth up his enemies round about. His lightnings enlightened the world: the earth saw, and trembled. The hills melted like wax at the presence of the LORD, at the presence of the Lord of the whole earth. The heavens declare his righteousness, and all the people see his glory (vv. 1-6).

These are responses from creation.

Creation will recognize Him when He returns. An important message is given by Paul in Romans 8: "For we know that the whole creation groaneth and travaileth in pain together until now . . . waiting for the redemption of our body" (vv. 22-23). Creation will respond to the coming of Christ, even as creation responded to His first coming.

The glory of the Lord was prophesied, as the prophets told what would be accomplished at His coming; His glory was pictured on the mount of transfiguration; and His glory will be perceived by creation. How should this affect us? In Psalm 2 the psalmist says: "Serve the LORD with fear, and rejoice with trembling. Kiss the Son, lest he be angry, and ye perish from the way. . . . Blessed are all they that put their trust in him" (vv. 11-12).

In realization that Jesus Christ is coming back to establish

His Kingdom, we ought to submit to Him. Each one should be certain that in his life the Lord Jesus Christ has first place, that He is really King of kings and Lord of lords. Peter exhorted in Acts 3:19: "Repent ye therefore, and be converted, that your sins may be blotted out when the times of refreshing shall come from the presence of the Lord." As Peter spoke primarily to Jewish people, he proclaimed the need of repentance. You need to change your mind about Jesus, because He is the Lord, He is the Son of God, and He is going to come back.

Prophecy, given to glorify God, intends to reveal the wonderful character of Jesus Christ. When He returns, His glory is going to be seen, enjoyed, and appreciated, and all will worship at His feet.

13

Will Israel Possess the Promised Land?

JOHN F. WALVOORD

THE QUESTION of whether Israel will ever possess their promised land is being considered a great deal in our day, especially so in view of the fact that twenty-six years ago the nation Israel was officially formed. It has grown and increased its territory and strength over the last quarter of a century. The question is more than simply an item in prophecy. In many respects, this question is the key to understanding the entire Word of God. Perhaps alongside it is the important question of whether God's promises are true.

In the Scriptures, the promises given to Israel begin with God's dealings with Abraham. Abraham was reared in Ur of Chaldees, a city in southern Mesopotamia not too far from Babylon. Archaeology has located it and has demonstrated that life was there at a high cultural level. But Ur of Chaldees was a wicked, pagan city.

To Abram, living in the darkness of Ur of Chaldees, God delivered a message. He told him to leave his home and kindred and go to a place chosen for him. And Abram, at least in partial obedience to God, began the long journey. He went northwest to the land of Haran. There he settled down with his father and his nephew Lot until his father died. Then appar-

126

ently God spoke to him again, and Abram eventually came to the promised land.

God had given him some very wonderful promises, called the Abrahamic covenant, first recorded in the early verses of Genesis 12. In the covenant is the promise that he would be a great man, that he would be the father of a great nation, and that through him all nations would be blessed. These promises subsequently had amazingly accurate fulfillment.

The very fact that Abraham is known four thousand years later is proof of the greatness of this man that God so used. That he was the father, not only of Israel but also of other nations, is a matter of history. The promise that through him would come blessing to all the world has already been amazingly and literally fulfilled. Through Abram came the nation of Israel; through Israel came the prophets; through the prophets, the writers of the Old Testament Scriptures and later the New Testament, by inspiration of God.

But over and beyond the revelation of God given through the prophets orally and through the Scriptures, there was a supreme presentation to the world of the gift of God's Son, born of Jewish blood, as the Scriptures had predicted, through the line of Abraham, Isaac, and Jacob, the tribe of Judah, and the family of David. Truly, the promises to Abraham have in large measure already been fulfilled. But in these promises, and implicit in their ultimate fulfillment, is the promise of the land.

In Genesis 12:1, God told Abram to "Get thee out of thy country, and from thy kindred, and from thy father's house, unto a land that I will show thee." When he got to the land, the Lord appeared unto Abram and said, "Unto thy seed will I give this land" (12:7). It may seem rather strange that Christians, mostly of Gentile background, should have any interest in a promise given to the seed of Abraham that they will some day possess the land. But the promise is tremendously significant. It is the key to what unfolds in the rest of the Bible, including the consummation in Christ's future Kingdom on earth.

Not everyone has approached this promise in the same way. Many today raise the question, "Is this promise true?" We live in a day when the Bible is disregarded, when even in some theological seminaries it is no longer considered the Word of God. The first problem in a text like this is the question, "Is the promise true?"

The Bible has demonstrated it is the Word of God in many ways. Among them is the evidence of meticulous fulfillment of prophecy in hundreds of instances, a fact that sets the Bible apart from any other book. This Book alone, of all world literature, is inspired of the Holy Spirit. It is the Word of God. For those who trust Christ and have accepted the promises of salvation, this promise, on the face of it, must be a true promise.

But this does not stop the critics of this particular promise. They say, "Yes, it is true, but, certainly it is not literally true. The land is just a symbol of heaven, and when the Old Testament promises a land, it is simply stating that believers in Christ will ultimately go to heaven." This is the nonliteral interpretation.

The term *land,* however, used in the Bible, means exactly what it says. It is not talking about heaven; it is talking about a piece of real estate in the Middle East. After all, if all God was promising Abraham was heaven, he could have stayed in Ur of Chaldees. Why go the long journey? Why be a pilgrim and a wanderer? No, God meant land, and we are going to see that in the subsequent promise.

Then there are those who say, "Yes, the Word of God is true, and it meant land, but the promise is a conditional promise. It depended upon the faithfulness of the people of God in obeying Him. Israel disobeyed God; therefore, the promise will not be fulfilled."

This is an interesting approach, because Israel on many occasions did disobey God. It is also clear that for many generations it meant they were not to possess the land. But the question is still unresolved whether, in spite of all the departures from the faith of God's people in the Old Testament, and in spite of the delays to the fulfillment of His promise, the question is still, "Does the Bible promise God will give His people, Israel, the promised land?"

The promises of the land are not new. But the very number of them seems to indicate God anticipated that people would not accept these promises at face value. God repeated the promises again and again in such contexts and in such ways that it not only demonstrates the promise is true, that a literal land was promised, but it also demonstrates it is unconditional, in the sense of certainty of fulfillment.

It is God's purpose, in spite of human failure, ultimately to give the land to Israel. If this can be demonstrated, the question will be raised, "What is the significance of the present occupation of only a portion of the land by the people of Israel?" This is the question which faces us in our day.

There is almost a monotonous repetition of the promise of the land. The promise is repeated when Lot and Abram separate. "And the Lord said to Abram . . . lift up now thine eyes and look from the place where thou art, northward, southward, eastward and westward: for all the land which thou seest, to thee will I give it, and to thy seed forever" (Gen 13:14-15).

In Genesis 15 God began to deal with Abram concerning his seed, for he had no child. Again, God confirmed the covenant, this time with blood. A solemn sacrifice and a ceremony were carried out in which the promise of God was confirmed by the solemn oath of God. "In the same day the Lord made a covenant with Abram saying, Unto thy seed have I given this land, from the river of Egypt unto the great river, the river Euphrates" (Gen 15:18).

Although there *are* symbols in the Bible, to describe heaven as the area between the river of Egypt and the river Euphrates is strange, to say the least, especially when you read in the next few verses the names of all the heathen tribes who possessed the area. They are hardly symbols of the saints in glory. In fact, they were the nations that God was going to destroy. In the Bible, a symbol should correspond to the reality of the truth it represents, and the land does not correspond to heaven. It is the land from the river of Egypt to the river Euphrates. Abram regarded this as a piece of real estate, an earthly promise God was pledging Himself to fulfill.

It is true that in Hebrews we are told Abraham "looked for a city which hath foundations, whose builder and maker is God" (11:10). I am sure he did. Abraham eventually will dwell in the New Jerusalem, as all the saints will. But this does not contradict the fact He will fulfill the promise of the land first, before the earth is destroyed and before the new heaven and the new earth are created.

This promise of the land is repeated again and again. Genesis 17:8 reads, "I will give unto thee and to thy seed after thee, the land wherein thou art a stranger, all the land of Canaan, for an everlasting possession; and I will be their God." In Genesis 26:3-4 the promise is repeated to Isaac. The promise was not given to all the descendants of Abraham, but the promise was given to the line of Isaac. In Genesis 28 the promise is repeated to Jacob. It was not given to Esau, but to Jacob. Jacob was the father of the twelve tribes of Israel to whom the promise of the land is given in the Word of God.

When we study these portions of Scripture, one significant fact stands out—Abraham never possessed the land, Isaac never possessed the land, and Jacob never possessed the land. It is evident the promise of possession of the promised land was not something to be fulfilled immediately. Instead, in Genesis 15 God told Abraham that his seed, yet unborn, was going to a strange land and for hundreds of years would live outside the promised land. Then God predicted in Genesis 15:13-14 they would return as a great people.

Did God mean this? Subsequent Scriptures record how in Joseph's time they went down into Egypt, a family of some seventy people, and remained there for hundreds of years and grew from a small group to a nation of probably more than two million. It was then that God called Moses, Aaron, and Joshua, and the children of Israel left Egypt. After their forty years wandering in the wilderness, they returned to possess the land. Moses reminded them of this in Deuteronomy 11:22-25, even though he himself never possessed any portion of the land west of the Jordan.

Joshua, as he faced the task that was his after Moses' death, records in Joshua 1:1 this same promise that God had granted them the land. Every portion of the land they put their foot on would be theirs. Subsequently, beginning at Jericho and Ai, they began to conquer the land.

Before Moses died, however, he solemnly warned the children of Israel that if they did not obey the law, they would be driven from the land; and in the solemn series of blessings and curses recorded in Deuteronomy, the second law, Moses summed up a final word to the children of Israel. He plainly told them that because of their sins they would be driven out of the land and dispossessed again.

Subsequently this happened. The years rolled on. Israel survived the apostasy of the judges. They rose to the splendor of the kingdom under Saul, David, and Solomon. Under Solomon much of the land came under Israel's control, though not entirely possessed. Solomon placed it under tribute. But Solomon disobeyed the Word of God. He multiplied horses and instruments of war; he multiplied wives who bore his children and reared them without faith in the God of Israel. After Solomon's death the kingdom was divided between the two tribes around Jerusalem, Judah and Benjamin, and the ten tribes called the kingdom of Israel, led entirely by ungodly kings. In keeping with the warning God gave through Moses and later repeatedly through the prophets, they were driven out of the land.

The Assyrians came in 721 B.C. and carried captive the ten tribes. They did not succeed in reducing Jerusalem, however.

Then about 125 years later, in 605 B.C. Nebuchadnezzar, the general of the Babylonian armies, conquered Jerusalem. About the same time, through his father's death, he became king of Babylon. It was he who led Daniel and others into captivity. In subsequent years they depopulated the land and ultimately destroyed Jerusalem and the temple in 586 B.C., leaving Jerusalem in ruins and Israel once again out of the land. But the promise of the land still persisted; even in the height of Israel's apostasy in Jeremiah's day when their city was to be destroyed, God gave them a word of assurance: "For thus saith the Lord, after seventy years are accomplished at Babylon, I will visit you and perform my good work toward you in causing you to return even unto this place" (Jer 29:10). God had predicted they would go down into Egypt, and they did. He had foretold they would return to the land and they did. He had predicted if they forsook the Law they would be driven out of the land, and they were. But now He predicts they will return.

It was many years later that somehow this prophecy came into the hands of Daniel. Daniel had been carried off to Jerusalem, probably in the fall of 605 B.C., shortly after Nebuchadnezzar conquered the city. In Babylon, wicked city of the ancient world, he had maintained a spotless life of purity, and had distinguished himself as an administrator under Nebuchadnezzar and subsequent kings. Daniel had lived long enough to see some of these prophecies fulfilled. Babylon had fallen as Daniel said it would (chapter 5). The Medes and the Persians had now taken over.

In the first year of Darius, who reigned in Babylon in the Medo-Persian empire, Daniel came into possession of the book of Jeremiah. As he read the stirring prophecy of Jeremiah, so amazingly fulfilled in the destruction of Jerusalem and the captivity of Israel, his heart leaped as he came to the promise in Jeremiah 29:10 that after seventy years they would return to Jerusalem. Why was he excited? About sixty-seven to sixty-eight years had already elapsed.

A glimpse of the heartache of Daniel in relation to Jerusalem and the land of Israel is revealed in Daniel 6 when he was thrown into the lion's den for praying to God. It was his custom to look three times a day toward Jerusalem still in ruin, and pray. He was a busy administrator, but he never forgot the city of God. After all these years of praying for the peace of Jerusalem, he now realized God was soon to answer his prayers.

While Daniel himself was too old to go back, now probably about eighty, and occupied with duties in Babylon, Ezra records how 50,000 went back. In spite of delays, after twenty years the Temple was finally rebuilt about 516 B.C. It was not until much later, when Nehemiah came in 445 B.C. several generations later, that the walls of Jerusalem were rebuilt, the debris of the city carried out, and by lot one out of ten was chosen to build his home in the city of Jerusalem.

In the next fifty years after Nehemiah, Jerusalem became once again the headquarters for Israel's government, and the people of Israel were again in the land. When Jesus Christ was born, as the prophets had predicted, he was not born in Babylon, but in Bethlehem, a little town south of Jerusalem. While Israel had failed, and God had fulfilled His predicted judgments upon them, it was also true God was not content until His people were back in the land.

But there were the promises to Abraham and Moses, and those through the prophets who predicted there was still a delay in the ultimate fulfillment of the promise. Moses had not only predicted they would be driven out of the land, but also in Deuteronomy 28:64 is a sad picture of Israel scattered over the world in persecution, in fear of their lives, unsettled, without peace and rest, because they would not listen to the Word of God. In due time this promise also was fulfilled.

Christ solemnly warned His disciples the beautiful Temple Herod was building for the children of Israel was to be destroyed. Begun fifteen years before Christ was born, it was not completed until more than thirty years after His death.

This Temple, magnificent in its construction of stones quarried from the city of Jerusalem, and built in beautiful dimensions impressive even in Christ's day, was to be destroyed. Not one stone would be left upon another.

This sad prediction of Christ's was fulfilled in A.D. 70 when Jerusalem, crowded with Jewish pilgrims who had come for the feasts, was surrounded by Roman soldiers. The Romans slaughtered them in an awful massacre. The city was set to the torch, and the stones of the Temple were literally pried loose, so that no stone was left upon another.

Jerusalem today has the Wailing Wall, but it is not a wall of the Temple itself. In recent excavations of the southeast corner of Jerusalem some of the very stones that were cast into the valley below when the Temple was destroyed have been recovered. The stones had hit with such force they not only shattered but also shattered the rocks they hit. The evidence is there, a mute testimony to the accuracy of the prophetic word.

Following A.D. 70, in a methodical persecution the Roman government drove Israel out of the land. Their cities, crops, and wells were destroyed. The land was left almost uninhabitable. And, precisely as Moses had said, they were scattered all over the world.

It would not be difficult to find learned scholars who a generation ago asserted dogmatically that Israel would never go back to their ancient land. The nation might experience spiritual revival; they might join the Christian Church by faith; but they would never go back to the land. Scholars felt this promise could not be fulfilled, because Israel had rejected Messiah as their final opportunity.

But not so with the Word of God. For the same Word which predicted that Israel would go to Egypt and return, was literally fulfilled; the same Word which foretold they would be carried off by the Assyrians and Babylonians and then return, was exactly fulfilled; the same Word which declared the temple would be destroyed and they would be scattered all over the earth, was literally fulfilled; that same Word of God predicted they would be regathered from over the world.

These prophecies are found all through the major and minor prophets. By way of illustration, consider Jeremiah: "Lo, the days come, saith the LORD, that I will bring again the captivity of my people Israel and Judah, saith the LORD: I will cause them to return to the land that I gave to their fathers, and they shall possess it" (30:3). Then he went on to say that after they return, they will be plunged into a time of travail and trouble. He warns them: "Alas! for that day is great, so that none is like it: it is even the time of Jacob's trouble, but he shall be saved out of it" (v. 7). In other words, they will be regathered, brought back to their ancient land. They will suffer purging judgments from God, but will be saved and delivered from their enemies. He goes on to say, "It shall come to pass in that day, saith the LORD of hosts, that I will break his yoke from off thy neck, and will burst thy bonds, and strangers shall no more serve themselves of him. But they shall serve the LORD their God, and David their king, whom I will raise up unto them" (vv. 8-9).

When Jeremiah spoke these words, David had been dead for five or six hundred years. Here he prophesied the resurrection of David. This is going to occur at the second coming of Jesus Christ. He predicted they would "serve the LORD their God and David their king, whom I will raise up unto them." This is one of several instances in the Old Testament that referred to David as resurrected and as serving as prince, or subruler, under Christ in His future millennial Kingdom. God, through Jeremiah, told Israel not to be dismayed: "I may destroy all the nations, but I will never destroy the nation of Israel" (v. 10). God will fulfill His promise. He will give the land to Israel forever.

In Jeremiah and other prophets this promise is repeated again. Jeremiah 31:8 ff. states they will come from all directions, from the north country and from the farthest part of the earth. In Jeremiah 32 additional promises are given and are stated over and over in the major and minor prophets.

In Ezekiel 39:28 the return of Israel to the land is mentioned: "Then shall they know that I am the LORD their God which caused them to be led into captivity among the heathen, but I have gathered them unto their own land, and have left none of them anymore there." The ultimate promise is that every true Israelite will be gathered and brought back to the promised land.

Ezekiel 20 tells us they will be subject to a purging judgment, but those counted worthy will be brought back from all over the world to their promised land. This, of course, will occur in the millennial Kingdom.

The prophecy of Amos, for the most part an indictment of Israel for their sin, predicts the revival of Israel and indicates, "I will bring again the captivity of my people of Israel, and they shall build the waste cities, and inhabit them; and they shall plant vineyards and make wine thereof; they shall also make gardens and eat the fruit of them" (9:14). This has already been fulfilled, to some extent. But he says further, "And I will plant them upon their land, and they shall no more be pulled up out of their land which I have given them, saith the Lord thy God" (v. 15). Yes, they went down to Egypt out of the land and came back. Yes, they went into captivity and came back. Yes, they were scattered all over the world, but God says they are coming back. And when they come back, they will never be scattered again.

Now, the question is, "Has this been fulfilled?" The answer is no. The children of Israel have not been restored. These promises have not been completely fulfilled. What we see today is something that is most amazing. But it is the first phase of what I regard as a fourfold program leading to Israel's ultimate restoration. These steps are logical; they are chronological; and they have a cause-and-effect relationship. What we see today is the first stage.

According to Scripture, first of all, Israel has to go back to the land. They have to be organized as a political state, because the Scriptures record that in the last days prior to the second coming of their Messiah to the earth, they will make a covenant with a king who will arise in the Middle East. It will be a covenant designed for a seven-year fulfillment (Dan 9: 27). It is a most significant covenant because at the end of the seven years Jesus Christ will return to bring in His Kingdom. It should be obvious this covenant could not be signed unless Israel was back in the land, organized as a political state, and in a situation where they needed Gentile protection and agreement—precisely the condition of Israel today.

This will be followed by a second phase. When the covenant is signed, it apparently will bring in a time of peace. It is mentioned sometimes, especially in Ezekiel 38, that there will be a period when Israel will rest securely and in safety. Under the supposed protection of this Gentile ruler, yet to appear, they are going to have the second phase of safety. I assume, in that period, multiplied thousands of Jews from all over the world will flock to their ancient land supposing at long last now they have a home land safe and secure.

But their hope is short-lived. For the Scriptures indicate after three and a half years the covenant will be broken. Following their period of peace they will enter into a period of persecution (Jer 30), the time of Jacob's trouble which Daniel refers to in Daniel 12:1 as the time of great tribulation, and which Christ referred to as the Great Tribulation in Matthew 24, when He warned the children of Israel to flee to the mountains of Judea. Obviously, Israel has to be in Judea in order to flee to the mountains of Judea. The book of Revelation calls this time the Great Tribulation, the day of God's wrath, for it is a time of judgment upon a Christ-rejecting world. This is the third period.

The fourth period will come when Jesus Christ Himself returns in power and glory. Then the promises of regathering will be fulfilled. Every Israelite, from all over the world, will be brought back, not by choice, but by order of Christ Himself, to their ancient land. Those counted worthy will be established in the millennial Kingdom. They will possess the land from the river of Egypt to the river Euphrates, and they will possess the land forever, that is, as long as the earth lasts, until the earth itself is destroyed and the new heaven and new earth are created.

What we see today is the first phase. But it is obvious we could not have the second phase without the first; nor the third phase without one and two; nor the fourth, or millennial stage, without this natural progression. If fifty thousand Jews who went back from Babylon to the promised land fulfilled the promise of the second regathering, it seems obvious that almost three million Jews now in the Holy Land are not just an accident. This is the most significant movement of the people of Israel since the days of Moses. And it sets the stage for end-time events.

From our standpoint as Christians it is tremendously significant. The first phase is already complete, and Israel is a nation. But the second phase, the covenant phase, in my understanding of prophecy, cannot come until after the rapture of the Church. We wait the upward call. But once the Church is gone, the lawless one, the dictator of the Middle East—eventually to be a world ruler—will appear in history and make his covenant with Israel. And Scripture will be methodically fulfilled, second phase, third phase, fourth, and glorious restoration of the people of Israel to their ancient land.

Just as certainly as God will fulfill His promises to Israel, He will fulfill His promises to His Church. If there ever was an hour in which men should put their trust in the Lord—first of all for salvation, but then in all the glorious promises of God—it is the hour in which we live. Yes, God will keep His promises for Israel. But He is also going to fulfill His promises for every believer.

14

The Glory Hour of Israel

CHARLES LEE FEINBERG

ONE OF THE MOST heartening themes of all prophecy, in view of the sad and troublous past of God's people Israel, is the glory hour of Israel. The student of Scripture immediately meets with an embarrassment of riches when he approaches this subject of prophecy. Prophet after prophet delights to foretell the hour of Israel's glorious consummation. But no prophet in the Old Testament pictures the glories of Israel's future in more glowing and beautiful terms than the prophet Isaiah . Such a passage is Isaiah 59:20—60:3:

> And the Redeemer shall come to Zion, and unto those who turn from transgression in Jacob, saith the LORD. As for me, this is my covenant with them, saith the LORD; My Spirit that is upon thee, and my words which I have put in thy mouth, shall not depart out of thy mouth, nor out of the mouth of thy seed, nor out of the mouth of thy seed's seed, saith the LORD, from henceforth and forever. Arise, shine; for thy light is come, and the glory of the LORD is risen upon thee. For, behold, the darkness shall cover the earth, and gross darkness the peoples, but the LORD shall arise upon thee, and his glory shall be seen upon thee. And the nations shall come to thy light, and kings to the brightness of thy rising.

From beginning to end in the passage before us there runs the tremendously exhilarating, uplifting, strengthening theme of glory. It is difficult to imagine how a reader of Scripture is impressed by the passage just quoted, but it is sufficient to elevate the spirit in praise of God. As one thinks of the harried, persecuted people of Israel, driven from pillar to post with no place to lay their heads, the text comes with great comfort and force. Said a writer, "Mankind has its resting-place, but Israel only the grave."

It must be emphasized that, when we say Isaiah dilates and enlarges on Israel's glory, we do not imply that he glosses over their sins. There is no veneer of their sin with Isaiah. Listen to him.

> The ox knoweth his owner, and the ass, his master's crib, but Israel doth not know; my people doth not consider. Ah, sinful nation, a people laden with iniquity, a seed of evildoers, children that are corrupters; they have forsaken the LORD, they have provoked the Holy One of Israel unto anger, they are gone away backward (Is 1:3-4).

He is the prophet who directly leveled the accusation against God's people: "But we are all as an unclean thing, and all our righteousnesses are as filthy rags; and we all do fade as a leaf, and our iniquities, like the wind, have taken us away" (Is 64: 6). (For an extended indictment of their evil doings see Is 5:8-23.) But one of the grandest of his portrayals of future glory for Israel is found in the portion under consideration.

The passage is preceded by a section dealing with a call to repent, the revelation of Jacob's transgression, Israel's confession, and the Lord's answer in His personal appearing. The Redeemer's coming (59:20) is now likened to the appearing of light. As with a trumpet call Isaiah exhorts Israel: "'Arise, shine; for thy light is come, and the glory of the LORD is risen upon thee" (60:1). It is the voice of the prophet calling to his people, more particularly to Jerusalem. The Greek Old Testament and the Latin Vulgate insert the word *Jerusalem*. But that is quite unnecessary, because the words "arise" and "shine" and the pronoun suffix in "thy light" are all feminine in the original language. They relate to the city of Jerusalem, the beloved city of God, the city of the great King.

But notice that she is told to arise. What is her physical condition? You may find it clearly depicted in Isaiah 51:23: "But I will put it [the cup of God's fury just mentioned in v. 22] into the hand of those who afflict thee, who have said to thy soul, bow down, that we may go over; and thou hast laid thy body like the ground, and like the street, to those who went over." This has been Israel's position for time beyond telling. The nations who have persecuted her have used her as a door mat. She had no choice in the matter. To the same effect are the words in 52:1-2. Seated in the dust with bands about her neck, Jerusalem is enjoined to loose herself. This is liberation for her who has been so long mentally and physically distraught.

Jerusalem with such a past the prophet urges to give forth the light she has now received, to reflect it to the glory of God. It is not light from the blinding flash of the atom or hydrogen bomb. Recent writings indicate the effects of the first detonation of the atom bomb. They know what damage was caused by way of heat and blast five miles away, ten miles, up to thirty miles away, but that is not the kind of light indicated here. But there is something more. It is the Lord Himself who made the sun, the Sun of righteousness who rises, as Malachi predicts, with healing in His wings. It will be the Lord God Himself, the Messiah of Israel. And what is the need for such a display? Because Israel does not have this light. Have you noticed how valueless much in creation is without light? What do the colors in creation, the grass, the sun with its sunrise and sunset, mean to a person without light? What does the most beautiful work of art in the galleries of the world signify without light? All these are valueless without light.

Their light has come according to God's faithful promise.

Messiah has returned to Israel in the hour of her darkest need. He said He would come, and He has come. Zechariah 12 and 14 foretell that all nations will come against Jerusalem. Then the Lord will go forth in that day and fight as He did in the day of Midian. His feet will stand in that day upon the Mount of Olives east of Jerusalem, and the mountain will be split latitudinally for a way of escape for the beleaguered people of Israel. The hour will find them in their greatest need. The nations of earth will be in well-aligned, well-defined confederacies. Then Christ will say, "Now is My time to take over. The world has too long been unmindful that Israel has a Champion. It is the Holy One of Israel, I, the Lord Jesus Christ."

How do we know that? The latter part of Isaiah 60:1 tells us that. The glory of the Lord, not that of some man, but the glory of the Lord will have risen. Someone has said with reference to the east, "The sun does not rise; it leaps over the horizon." That Dayspring from on high (Lk 1) who visited earth in the first advent comes as light in the second advent. The text before us pictures a city gleaming in the rays of the dawning sun. How blessed it is to have the light!

The incident is told of a minister going to Helena, who saw piles of boxes and goods and all manner of things on the landing. He said to the superintendent, "Do the slaves buy as much as used to be purchased for them by their owners?"

The answer was, "A great deal more."

"Well, what things do they buy?" was the second question.

"Buy? Looking-glasses and candles."

"Looking-glasses, of course; but candles?" he asked. "What do they want with candles?"

It was explained that in the old slave days a slave was never allowed to have a lighted candle in his cabin after dark; nothing, unless it was a fire, was allowed. The candles became, in their eyes, the symbol of liberty. The moment they were free, they said, "Give us light."

The very light of God Himself (1 Jn 1:5) will be Israel's in that day.

Now notice the darkness. Before the return of Messiah the testimony of the nation is clear:

> Therefore is justice far from us, neither does righteousness overtake us. We wait for light, but behold obscurity; for brightness, but we walk in darkness. We grope for the wall like the blind, and we grope as if we had no eyes; we stumble at noonday as in the night; we are in desolate places like dead men (Is 59:9-10).

The light is longed for and looked for, because earth does not furnish it. Rather, the earth is covered, as it were, with a total blackout. Gross, heavy darkness envelopes the peoples of earth.

Never mistake it that the light furnished proceeds from the nations of earth. The prophet speaks of the world's alienation from God. It will assuredly be dark in that day because of the unleashing of the forces of evil and the culmination of the mystery of iniquity (2 Th 2:1-12; Rev 13)—all this before the glorious coming of Messiah to earth to rectify earth's wrongs and to reign in righteousness.

As Isaiah has announced in verse 1 the glory of the Lord has risen upon Jerusalem, so now in verse 2 he proclaims the Lord will arise upon her. When it is declared God's glory will be seen upon His city and people, it means more than that it will be visible; it will be conspicuous and preeminent. It will be bright and luminous to be seen from a great distance like a glory cloud as in ancient days of desert wandering. We are reminded of the light foretold in Isaiah 9:2 and the light Israel enjoyed in Egypt when darkness covered the homes of the Egyptians. You will recall the first creative command from God was the separation of darkness from light (Gen 1:2-3). Paul draws the beautiful analogy in the spiritual realm in 2 Corinthians 4:6. The Lord is both a sun and shield (Ps 84:11).

Undoubtedly, the world loves darkness rather than light, but God promises to dispel earth's dark night.

It is told that a colonial governor of the Bahamas, about to return to England, offered his services to obtain from the home government any favor the colonists might wish. The unanimous answer was both unexpected and surprising. They said: "Tell them to tear down the lighthouses; they are ruining the prosperity of this colony." The colonists wanted ships to be wrecked upon the reefs in order to rob the goods they contained. Earth's favorite atmosphere is darkness, but God intends to remove it in that day. And He will.

If verse 1 of our passage is beautiful and verse 2 builds on it, then unquestionably verse 3 is the capstone. It speaks of the light for the nations. Whenever you read in the Scriptures that Israel is blessed, do not be envious of them. God blesses them in order that the nations of earth may be blessed through them. Foolish beyond words is jealousy which inquires why God chose Israel. God initiated that in Abraham's Son and descendants all the families of the earth might be blessed.

What would you think of a man who gathered firewood for his hearth, set it ablaze, partook of its light and warmth, then suddenly became enraged at the burning timbers? He would have lost all sense of the realities of the situation, for the logs were burning for his warmth and pleasure. The text states clearly the nations and their kings would be attracted to Jerusalem's light and to the brightness of her rising. It is ever so: Israel's light means light for the world. Read Romans 11, and see how Israel's light and restoration to God's favor spell out life from the dead for the world (v. 15). Hear the word in Psalm 67:1-2, 7, which gives the heart of the missionary thrust: "God be merciful unto us, and bless us; and cause his face to shine upon us; Selah. That thy way may be known upon earth, thy saving health among all nations. . . . God shall bless us; and all the ends of the earth shall fear him."

The same truth is set forth in the pivotal passage in Acts 15.

James was stating the old truth: Israel blessed means the residue of the nations will be enriched spiritually.

When will we learn that the only hope for light for the dark world is the light reflected when Israel is in the place of blessing and glory? One godly expositor put it well: "Only when Israel is restored will whole nations receive the light of Divine testimony and acknowledge the truth relating to the living God and His Christ." The Gentiles will come because they will be attracted to and by that glory. One of the most dramatic confirmations of this truth in Isaiah is found in Zechariah 8:22, 23:

> Yea, many peoples and strong nations shall come to seek the Lord of hosts in Jerusalem, and to pray before the Lord. Thus saith the Lord of hosts: In those days it shall come to pass that ten men shall take hold out of all languages of the nations, even shall take hold of the skirt of him that is a Jew, saying, We will go with you; for we have heard that God is with you.

Is it not immediately discernible that there is an unbreakable relationship between Israel and blessing for the world?

Moreover, the mention of Jerusalem's rising reveals that the city itself has become a luminary (see Rev 21:24). Notice the reference to the coming of the kings. This verse is the basis for the legend that the magi (great ones) of Matthew 2:1 were kings. Thus, we find here the important relation between receiving the light and giving it forth.

One night a motorist was killed by a train at a grade crossing. The old signalman in charge of the crossing had to appear in court. After a prolonged and severe cross examination, he still stood his ground. He said he had waved his lantern frantically, but to no avail.

The following day the superintendent of the company called him into his office. He said, "You did wonderfully well yesterday, Tom. I was afraid at first that you might waver under cross examination."

"No, sir," said the old gentleman, "but I was afraid that old

lawyer was going to ask me whether or not my lantern was lit!"
How necessary it is to have the light reflected and shining.

We used to sing an old missionary hymn in our student days:

> Shall we whose souls are lighted
> With wisdom from on high;
> Shall we to souls benighted
> The lamp of life deny?

How can we deny this light to Israel? And to the many other benighted areas of the world? This is true even in Jerusalem today. In that great city there is more religion by the square inch than exists in most parts of the world by the square mile, but so little Gospel as to be scarcely recognizable. The hour is an urgent one for men and women the world over.

Do you have that light? It is impossible to reflect it if you do not possess it. We know Satan is in the business of blinding the eyes of the unsaved lest the glorious light is received by faith. Trust Him now to illumine your heart in answer to faith. Then it will be your glory hour, not for time alone, but for eternity.

15

The Future Divine Regathering of Israel

S. Maxwell Coder

During the great excitement caused by the rebirth of the State of Israel, not many people noticed the general misunderstanding of its place in the program of God. It was hailed as a fulfillment of prophecy. But most Scriptures cited in support of this did not apply. The purpose of our study is to examine the actual words of the Bible dealing with the Jews and their land in the time of the end, so we can understand clearly the present return and the divine regathering which is to follow some day.

Godly men and women differ with regard to some of the difficult themes of Bible prophecy. But we can all agree on what the text actually states.

Three Departures from the Land

A necessary background is the fact that God's Word speaks of three departures from the land by the people of Israel, and three restorations. The first departure was the sojourn in Egypt for some four hundred years, followed by a return under the direct supervision of God (Gen 15:13-14; Ex 3:8). The second was the Babylonian captivity of seventy years, terminated by a divine restoration (Jer 29:10). The third is the present world dispersion, to be ended by a divine regathering after an unspecified length of time (Deu 28:64; 30:3).

In each case God acts to bring His people back to their land. The predicted miraculous return of world Jewry, which is to follow the return of Christ, has not yet taken place. What we have seen is something quite different, though it has been the most astonishing movement of the people of Israel since the Exodus from Egypt.

The Present Return

Two distinct groups of passages in the Bible have to do with the Jews and their land in the last days. The larger revelation predicts a stunning intervention in human affairs by God to restore His ancient people to their own land. The smaller revelation describes the land and its people before and during the seventieth week of Daniel 9:27. It is not, strictly speaking, a series of prophecies concerning a return to Palestine. It is rather a number of factual statements which reveal the presence of a large population of the people of Israel in Palestine as the Day of the Lord draws nigh, and as God's fury breaks over the land during the time of tribulation.

Out of a much larger revelation, let us look at four representative passages, beginning with Ezekiel 38-39. In this extended prophecy about a future invasion of the land by armies from the north, we read that the people who live there are called by the Lord "my people of Israel" (38:14). Although they are also referred to as "the people that are gathered out of the nations" (38:12), the text does not state God has gathered them in fulfillment of such prophecies, as we will examine later. Remarkably, in the light of present conditions in the land, they are said to be living without the protection of the walls found in ancient Palestine, and they are wealthy (38:11-12). How did these Jews get there? We are not told, but there they are in the land in "the latter years," "the latter days" (38:8, 16).

In order to make it clear that we are not reading here of the future divine regathering of Israel, let us anticipate a later part of this study. These Jews are not yet converted when the invasion takes place, because this seems to be described in Ezekiel 39:22, 29. They appear to be there in unbelief. More importantly, not until after God has destroyed the invaders does He say, "Now will I bring again the captivity of Jacob" (39:25). The time words in this and the following verses are of great importance.

The second chapter of Joel speaks of a similar situation. The time is said to be when the day of the Lord is coming, and is nigh at hand (2:1). The inhabitants of the land are called "children of Zion" (2:23). Their spiritual condition is seen in the exhortation by the Lord, "turn ye even to me with all your heart" (2:12), and in the fact that the heathen say, "Where is their God?" (2:17).

The Jews have made the land "as the garden of Eden" (2:3), but a northern army invades Palestine and desolates it (2:2-10). God intervenes and removes the invaders. It is "in those days, and in that time," that God is to "bring again the captivity of Judah and Jerusalem" (3:1), an expression referring to the divine restoration to the land. The judgment of the nations follows in Joel 3, and the establishment of the Kingdom as in Matthew 25.

The last three chapters of Zechariah tell us of the coming of the Day of the Lord, when Jerusalem will have become an international problem and will be attacked by all nations (12:2-3; 14:1-2). The Lord returns to the earth, and His feet stand upon the Mount of Olives. He delivers His people (14:3-5), who are five times called "the inhabitants of Jerusalem" (12:8). It is during this time that the Jews look upon Him whom they have pierced and mourn for Him (12:10). How they got to the land or when, we are not informed. But they have returned in unbelief. There seems to be nothing in Zechariah's description of conditions in Palestine in the day of the Lord which is unlike conditions in the land today.

In our Lord's great prophecy of Matthew 24-25, He spoke of the days before, during, and after the Great Tribulation (24:15-31). Here again we read that Palestine is inhabited by Jews, whom He calls "them which be in Judaea" (24:16). They are distinguished from the nations (24:9); they have a holy place (24:15); they observe the Sabbath (24:20) as do the Jews living there today. However, they are in the land in unbelief, because they betray one another; their love turns cold; there are false prophets and false Christs among them; and they seem to be distinguished from a smaller remnant called "the very elect" (24:10-12, 24). How did these Jews get to Palestine? The text is silent on this point, but it places the divine regathering of Israel, God's elect (Isa 45:4), afterward when the Lord returns (24:30-31). The Lord uses Old Testament language describing the dispersion when He says they will be brought from the four winds (Zech 2:6) and from one end of heaven to the other (Deu 30:4).

These passages found in Ezekiel, Joel, Zechariah, and Matthew are in agreement regarding the gathering of large numbers of Jews to inhabit Palestine in the end times, prior to the events which culminate in the divine restoration. It is such passages as these to which we must look for light upon the events of the present century which have witnessed the birth of the State of Israel.

THE DIVINE REGATHERING

The coming divine restoration of the Jews to their ancient homeland is a major theme of prophecy, mentioned in thirteen books of the Bible. At least twelve different words are used to describe it; thirty-five times we read that God will gather the Jews; thirty-five times it is written that He will bring them to their own land; twenty-three times the Scriptures speak of God turning, or bringing back, the captivity of Israel. He will recover them, assemble them, lead them back, place them, plant them in the land. Some texts refer to the regathering as an accomplished fact, "I have gathered them unto their own land" (Eze 39:28). All such passages are in striking contrast with the present return. When the Lord acts to restore His people, it will be after His return. Glory and great blessing will follow it. The Jews will receive a new heart; they will be cleansed from their iniquity. Every Jew in the world will be taken from the nations in an event described as a major miracle of God.

WHEN IT IS TO TAKE PLACE

So many time words, so many world-shaking events are mentioned in connection with the final end of the present world dispersion of the Jews. There can be no mistaking what the Bible teaches as to when it is to take place. It will be after the "many days" of Hosea 3:4-5, after Palestine has been taken over by a large population of Jews in the latter days, has been invaded by a northern confederacy of nations, and has witnessed a world-shaking divine intervention (Eze 38; 39:25). God will lead His people back after all nations have assembled against Jerusalem in the day of the Lord (Zec 14). The Great Tribulation must run its course before this takes place (Mt 24:21-31). The bringing back of Israel's captivity will follow a world-wide turning to God by the dispersed Jews and the second coming of Christ to the earth (Deu 30:1-5). Most of these texts make it clear that these events take place before the Kingdom is established (Zec 14:9; Mt 25:34).

THE SEQUENCE OF EVENTS

The order of events preceding and following the divine regathering is predicted first in the great prophecy of Deuteronomy 30:1-10. Something will make the Jews, scattered among the nations, remember God's words to Moses. They will "return unto the LORD" and obey His voice. It is then that the Lord will turn their captivity. He will return and gather them from the nations, bring them into their ancient homeland, change their hearts, and bless them while judging their enemies. Here are some of the factors involved:

1. The destruction of the invading armies described in Ezekiel 38-39 will be so appalling that all the nations will know this is an act of the God of Israel (38:16, 23; 39:21-23). While still scattered among those nations, "the house of Israel shall know that I am the LORD their God from that day and forward" (39:22).

2. The Gospel of the Kingdom will be preached in all the world for a witness to all nations (Mt 24:14). It is generally understood this will be done by the sealed 144,000 Jews of Revelation 7:1-8.

3. The ministry of the two witnesses of Revelation 11:3-12 will also have a world-wide impact upon Jews everywhere.

4. The testimony of Christian Jews as the Church age draws to a close, and Gospel literature to the Jews, will certainly make a deep impression on the people of Israel in all nations after the Church has been translated.

5. The mourning of all the tribes of the earth when they see the Son of Man coming in the clouds of heaven with power and great glory (Mt 24:30) specifically includes the Jews (Zec 12:10). Some believe the language used by our Lord actually limits this mourning to the tribes of Israel. Does the physical return of Christ complete the process by which world Jewry returns to the God of their fathers as predicted in Deuteronomy?

There issues from the hearts of the scattered Jews at that time a fervent prayer. "Save us, O LORD our God, and gather us from among the nations" (Ps 106:47; cf. Is 64:1). Their prayer is heard, and they come "with weeping, and with supplications" as the Lord leads them from all the coasts of the earth back to their land (Jer 31:8-9). As we read how the

Lord sends His angels to gather His elect, we find Him using the same language used in ancient times to describe their dispersion (Mt 24:31; Zec 2:6; Deu 30:4).

Not a single Jew is left behind (Eze 39:28). They are brought to "the wilderness of the people" where the rebels are screened out. Only the faithful, elsewhere called "the remnant," actually enter the land (Eze 20:34-38). A similar separation takes place among those who already live in Palestine (Zec 13:8, 9).

The miraculous character of this final regathering of Israel is not widely recognized. "Behold, the days come, saith the LORD, that it shall no more be said, The LORD liveth, that brought up the children of Israel out of the land of Egypt; but, The LORD liveth, that brought up the children of Israel from the land of the north, and from all the lands whither he had driven them: and I will bring them into their land that I gave unto their fathers (Jer 16:14-15; 23:7-8).

Throughout the Old Testament are scores of references to the exodus from Egypt (Num 15:41; Amos 2:10). It is the outstanding example in all history of the manifestation of God's power on Israel's behalf, when He worked with "signs, and with wonders, and with a strong hand, and with a stretched out arm, and with great terror" (Jer 32:21). Yet this future exodus of the Jews from all the nations of the world will be so remarkable a display of His power that the deliverance from Egypt will pale into insignificance in comparison.

It may also be said the present return of the Jews to Palestine will be forgotten when the Lord at last returns from heaven and fulfils His promise to restore His chosen nation to the land of their fathers.

16

Will Christ Reign on Earth 1000 Years?

JOHN F. WALVOORD

THE QUESTION as to whether Christ will reign on earth for a thousand years may seem at first glance to be quite irrelevant to the crying needs of our day—to the hustle and bustle of our cities, to our moral and political problems as they exist in the world today; perhaps many say this is something for the theologians to argue, that it does not have any vital bearing upon our personal Christianity, our winning of souls, or our testimony for Christ. I confess it is possible to study prophecy from a purely theoretical point of view and to spend a great deal of time discussing questions that are not of immediate moment to us. Not all aspects of prophecy are equally valuable.

It so happens, however, this particular question is more than just a question about a portion of theology or eschatology. As a matter of fact it is a key subject to unlock a whole principle of understanding the Bible. The question raised by this subject is a question as to whether we can interpret prophecy in its normal, literal sense. This brings us to a focal point in the portion of Scripture which expressly states Christ will reign on earth for a thousand years as found in Revelation 20. The opening verses of this chapter present a portion of divine truth which at first glance seems to teach Christ will return and bring in a Kingdom of one thousand years on earth.

In Revelation 19 there is a glorious revelation of the second coming of Jesus Christ, of His truimph over the forces of wickedness in the earth, His judgment of the world ruler and the false prophet, who are cast alive into the lake of fire, and His destruction of the armies gathered there in the Holy Land to fight it out for power. Immediately following this the apostle John records another revelation:

> I saw an angel come down from heaven, having the key of the bottomless pit and a great chain in his hand, and he laid hold on the dragon, that old serpent who is the devil and Satan, and bound him a thousand years, and cast him into the bottomless pit and shut him up and set a seal upon him that he should deceive the nations no more, till the thousand years should be fulfilled: and after that he must be loosed a little season. And I saw thrones and they sat upon them, and judgment was given unto them: and I saw the souls of them that were beheaded for the witness of Jesus, and for the word of God, and which had not worshipped the beast, neither his image, neither had received his mark upon their foreheads, or in their hands: and they lived and reigned with Christ a thousand years. But the rest of the dead lived not again until the thousand years were finished. This is the first resurrection. Blessed and holy is he that hath part in the first resurrection: on such the second death hath no power, but they shall be priests of God and of Christ, and shall reign with Him a thousand years (Rev 20:1-6).

The question in considering this passage is whether it means what it says, whether it is actually talking about a thousand-year period with certain events which precede, certain events which occur within the thousand years, and certain events which follow. If this is the correct interpretation, if we take this passage literally, then we must come to the conclusion that Christ when He comes to set up His kingdom will indeed reign on earth for 1000 years.

Biblical scholars, however, have not always agreed about how this chapter should be interpreted. Any fair analysis of early church history reveals the early Church Fathers clearly believed that Christ would return and reign on earth for a thousand years. The familiar quotation attributed to Justin Martyr who lived in the first part of the second century illustrates this. He said: "I and whatsoever Christians are orthodox in all things do know that there will be a resurrection of the flesh and a thousand years in the city of Jerusalem."

Then he enlarges upon his belief that Christ is coming back and will set up the Kingdom for a thousand years upon earth. Furthermore, he says this is the orthodox opinion. While there may have been currents of doctrine contrary to this in the early Church Fathers, it seems quite clear they believed Christ was going to reign on earth for a thousand years subsequent to His second coming.

In the course of church history, there arose in Alexandria in Egypt a new school of theology. It was headed up by such men as Clement of Alexandria and Origen and Gaius and others. They were quite enamored of the idealism of the philosophy of Plato, and attempted to combine Platonic philosophy with Christian theology. They thought that intellectual Christianity should be harmonized with Platonic philosophy, but they soon discovered that mixing Plato and the Bible was like mixing oil and water, and something had to give. They came up with the concept that the Bible was not intended to be interpreted literally, that it actually was a great allegory in which the real meaning was hidden and not the plain words of what the Scriptures taught.

By spiritualizing, or taking in a nonliteral sense what the Bible teaches in both the Old and New Testament, they somewhat succeeded in combining the theology of the Church with the philosophy of Plato, but to almost the total destruction of what we call orthodoxy.

The Alexandrian theologians were denounced as heretics by the early Church Fathers. There does not seem to have been anyone then or now to take very seriously this effort to make the whole Bible one great allegory which cannot be taken literally. I think there are few, if any, theologians, regardless of their theological background, who would defend the Alexandrian school of theology in its conclusion. But it did have a great impact upon the Church, especially in Africa.

Several generations later, the great theologian of the Roman Catholic church by the name of Augustine, the bishop of Hippo, came on the scene. In attempting to rescue biblical truth from the wreckage of African theology, which had followed in the wake of the Alexandrian school, he came up with a compromise. Namely, the Bible as a whole ought to be understood in its plain, ordinary sense, but prophecy was an exception; prophecy, at least most prophecy, should not be taken in its literal sense. He advocated what has been called the dual hermeneutic, or the dual principle of interpretation— interpreting the Bible in general literally, but interpreting prophecy in a nonliteral sense.

Using this method, although he did not defend it or support it by any considerable argument, Augustine decided that there was to be no millennial Kingdom, such as is defined in Revelation 20, and that actually we should look at this prophecy in a nonliteral sense. The millennial Kingdom was only a spiritual kingdom, rather than a literal kingdom on earth, and this spiritual kingdom was in some sense already in existence.

In the subsequent history of the Church, the view of Augustine was adopted, not only by the Roman Catholic church but also by the Protestant Reformers. While they recovered many of the precious truths related to Christianity that were lost in the Dark Ages—such as justification by faith, and every man his own interpreter of the Bible, and every Christian his own priest, and similar doctrines—they did very little to recover prophetic truth from the teaching of Augustine. Apart from removing the doctrine of purgatory and a few other Roman Catholic doctrines of this kind from the Protestant church, they did not tamper too much with Augustine's idea of the future. So there was perpetuated within the Protestant church a view that denies there will be a literal reign of Christ on earth, a view given the name amillennialism. In other words, they feel that while Christ may come back literally as the Bible indicates, when He comes back He will usher in immediately the eternal state and there will be no kingdom on earth. This view, of course, involves spiritualization of many Scriptures, as we will see.

Later in the history of the Protestant church came a man by the name of Daniel Whitby. He was not an orthodox theologian in many respects; he was a Unitarian. His writings were publicly burned. But he came out with still another view of the millennial Kingdom. Building upon the optimism of the theory of evolution—that the world is developing into a better and better world—he came up with the idea there would be a Millennium upon the earth, but it would not be a literal Millennium following the second coming of Christ. Rather, it would be an ideal social and political state brought in through preaching of the Gospel and through the influence and power of the Church. The world would be come Christianized, and there would come the time when missionary effort would reach its ultimate, and everyone would know the truth about Christ. The principles of Christianity would permeate and dominate the entire world. Then, Whitby held, at the conclusion of a thousand years of the triumph of the Gospel on earth, in which both Jews and Gentiles would be won to Christ in unprecedented numbers, Christ would come back to receive the triumphant Church and then usher in the eternal state. His view was called postmillennialism, meaning that the coming of Christ would follow a millennial kingdom on earth.

Although Daniel Whitby was a Unitarian, and in many respects a heretic, his views struck fire in his day and a number of orthodox theologians began to teach postmillennialism. It was quite a flourishing doctrine in the latter part of the nineteenth century and until World War I. It became increasingly evident, however, as the twentieth century continued, that the dream of Christianizing the world through the Church and the preaching of the Gospel was neither scriptural nor practical. History just was not going in that direction. Every day saw more people who had never heard the Gospel at all.

In many respects the Church was a receding force in the modern world as a whole, rather than a conquering, triumphant one. Postmillennialism died as a result of the events of the twentieth century, but it left in the field the two opposing views that (1) Christ *will* return and reign on earth for a thousand years, and (2) He will *not* reign on earth for a thousand years, and in a sense we are in the Kingdom period now.

The question as to which of these two views is right is not a question easily resolved. Some years ago I wrote a book entitled *The Millennial Kingdom,* in which I formally debated these views, including their historical backgrounds and their major theological concepts. As one gets into the doctrine, he discovers the whole question revolves around whether you can interpert prophecy literally.

One can go back as early as Genesis and ask the question, When God promised the land to Israel did He mean a literal land? It is true Israel left the land and went to Egypt, but they came back, as God said they would. It is true they went into the captivity, but they came back, as God said they would. Then they were scattered all over the world, as God said they would be. Are they coming back?

It would not be hard to find theologians who, a generation ago, issued dogmatic statements that Israel would never return to the land, never be restored. But history is against them today, because at least a portion of Israel is back in the land.

They have reestablished themselves as a nation. This seems to be the beginning of a grand movement to restore Israel literally as prophecy has given it to us.

As we examine other predictions in the Scriptures, such as the promise of the Kingdom to David, we find this, too, is not being fulfilled in any literal sense today. Only if Christ actually comes back and reigns on earth, can there be any literal fulfillment of the concept that the Davidic kingdom will be restored and that David himself will be resurrected and will serve under Christ as a number of Old Testament Scriptures indicate (Jer 30:9; Eze 34:23; 37:24). Also in the Old Testament is the prediction of a new covenant for Israel, a covenant to replace the Mosaic covenant. The new covenant guarantees Israel many spiritual blessings and predicts a time when every man will know the Lord, from the least to the greatest. This covenant cannot be literally applied to today. It requires a peculiar situation in the earth where Christ reigns, where everybody has the facts of the Gospel; then a literal fulfillment of this new covenant with Israel becomes possible.

But some writers say, "It is true the Old Testament taught a Kingdom on earth, that Christ would come back to found this Kingdom, that Israel would return to the land, but the New Testament does not support this." This becomes very interesting, especially when we come to Revelation 20, which is obviously New Testament truth.

As we trace through the gospel records we find the New Testament revelation exactly the same as the Old. In other words, the Old Testament which predicted a Kingdom on earth is also supported by the New Testament.

On one occasion the mother of James and John came to Christ and asked for a privilege. She wanted her two sons to sit on the right hand and on the left of Christ in His Kingdom. It is obvious she had in mind what the Old Testament prophecies predicted. Here would have been an ideal place for Christ to have expounded the doctrine that no literal fulfillment of these promises can be expected. Instead, knowing they would be, He said it was not His to give James and John the privilege of sitting on the right hand and on the left, but it would be given to those who were prepared for it. Earlier, in the announcement given to Mary that she was to be the mother of Messiah, the angel Gabriel recorded for her the wonderful promise that her Son would not only be born without a human father, conceived of the Holy Spirit, but that He would reign over the children of Israel forever (Lk 1:32-33). It seems clear Mary understood this to be in the literal sense the Old Testament prophecies had predicted—that her Son would actually reign over the house of Israel and fulfill the glorious promises given to the nation Israel.

As we move on through the New Testament, we find confirmation rather than contradiction. Another confirmation occurred when the Lord dealt with His disciples on the day of His ascension. They asked, as recorded in Acts 1:6-7, "Lord, wilt thou at this time restore again the kingdom to Israel?" Christ said unto them, "It is not for you to know the times or the seasons, which the Father has put in his own power." Then He went on to predict the power of the Spirit in the present age.

This would have been subterfuge on the part of our Lord, if as a matter of fact there was not going to be any Kingdom, if the hope of the disciples for a Kingdom on earth in which Israel would be prominent was vain. If such were the case, this was the time to straighten it out. Up to this moment the disciples still anticipated a literal Kingdom which they would share when Christ would reign on earth. In fact, He had announced to them they would sit on thrones, judging the twelve tribes of Israel.

Revelation 20 does not deal with an isolated prophecy that presents a new idea. This passage is the capstone of a dominant theme of the Old Testament—that the ultimate end of all history and of God's purposes for the Jew and the Gentile, was to bring them into an ideal political and spiritual situation where the Messiah of Israel would reign over the entire world. Psalm 72 tells us all kings will fall down and worship Him and all nations will serve Him—something obviously never fulfilled in any spiritual or literal sense up to this hour. Revelation 20 is specific and factual prophecy.

First of all, there is a logical and chronological connection between Revelation 20 and 19. Chapter 19 pictures the second coming of Christ, the destruction of the armies, and casting of the beast and false prophet into the lake of fire. Chapter 20 is in natural sequence. It is utterly impossible to place it before chapter 19, because it does not make sense unless Christ has actually returned. In other words, any fair approach to this chapter leads to the conclusion that what we have here is subsequent action. Chapter 20 continues the action of the nineteenth chapter, in which Christ returns in power and glory. In this situation where Christ has returned triumphantly, we learn in Revelation 20:1-3 of the binding of Satan.

In support of the millennial point of view, attempts are made to explain this passage as if Satan were bound at the first coming of Christ. The New Testament does not teach this. It indicates Satan is very active in our present world, deceiving the nations (Rev 16:14). Satan is described by the apostle Peter as "a roaring lion going about seeking whom he may devour" (I Pe 5:8). He is described by Paul as an angel of light who would deceive even the elect if this were possible (2 Co 11:14). He is a very active person, and the book of Revelation pictures him as continuing as an active person, condemning the just and falsely accusing the brethren (Rev 12:9-10), until he is finally cast out of heaven about three and a half years before the second coming of Christ. So it is obvious that he is very active in earth. There is no indication whatever that Satan is bound now.

This is a great embarrassment to the amillennial theologians. One, ordinarily quite sensible in theological pronouncements, concluded that Satan must be bound with a chain, but apparently it was a very long chain, because Satan is quite active.

Now, any fair examination of these verses does not indicate such a situation. If words mean anything at all, they indicate that during the thousand-year reign of Christ, Satan is wholly inactive. Notice again what it says. In his vision John saw an angel come down from heaven who had a key to the bottomless pit, which seems to be the home of the demons, and he had a great chain in his hand. This is what John saw.

As John watched, he saw the angel lay hold upon the dragon, the old serpent, who is the devil and Satan. Here we have four different titles so we can hardly miss the personage in view. Then the angel bound Satan for "a thousand years and cast him into the bottomless pit, and shut him up, and set a seal upon him, that he should deceive the nations no more till the thousand years should be fulfilled: and after that he must be loosed a little season" (Rev 20:2-3).

If words have any meaning at all, what is described here is rendering Satan completely inactive. It states he is bound. It says he is cast into the bottomless pit; it says a door is shut upon him, and the purpose is so he cannot deceive the nations any more until he is loosed again. If this is what the Scriptures teach, those who hold the amillennial view are wrong.

This series of actions requires a coming of Christ first, a binding of Satan, and a subsequent period of a thousand years in which Satan is bound, and other Scriptures relating to the millennial Kingdom are fulfilled. These three verses also illustrate an important principle of biblical interpretation, especially applicable to the Revelation; the principle is that in a symbolic presentation, as we have here, we must sharply distinguish between what a person sees and what he hears. What John saw was one whom he identified as an angel, and we assume this is correct. He saw the angel with a great chain in his hand and he saw him bind Satan; he saw him cast him into the pit; he saw him shut the door. That was all vision.

It is rather foolish to raise the question, as some say, "How can one bind Satan with a chain?" I am sure I could not do it, but if God set out to do it and used angelic agency, whatever the means might be, I believe God would be able to render Satan inoperative; that is what the Scripture indicates.

There were some things here that John could not see. He could not see, symbolically, the purpose of binding Satan. It had to be revealed to him. Why was Satan being bound? The purpose revealed to him was to render Satan inoperative, so he could not, as he had done in the years before the second coming of Christ, deceive the nations. This had to be revealed to John. Obviously, if it was revealed, it was intended to be interpreted literally.

Second, we learn from this passage that Satan is to be bound a thousand years. A thousand years is not subject to visual presentation. John could not see a thousand years. He had to be told how long Satan was going to be bound. This had to be a matter of direct revelation. Both the purpose and the length of the period during which Satan was bound are not symbolic in the presentation. It is an interpretation which God gave to the apostle John. On this basis we must take a thousand years literally. We must take the purpose literally; Satan is bound for a thousand years.

Subsequently, verse four describes a judgment. Here is an important segment of the argument, because this verse is absolute proof that Revelation 20 follows chronologically the preceding chapters. This is something which the amillennial view contradicts. They make the twentieth chapter a summary of all preceding chapters. The verse does not so indicate. As John wrote it down, he saw a throne, and they sat on them. He does not tell us who "they" were, and judgment was given unto them.

Now notice this, "I saw the souls of them that were beheaded for the witness of Jesus, and for the Word of God, who have not worshipped the beast, neither his image, neither have received his mark upon their forehead." When did these martyrs die?

They had died during the reign of the beast, in the period of three and a half years prior to the second coming of Christ. In other words, chapter 20 is a subsequent action. You could not very well raise people from the dead who had not been beheaded and who had not refused to worship the beast.

The very character of the martyred dead raised here indicates these are people who have died just before the second coming of Christ. If that is the case, their resurrection just after the second coming of Christ makes untenable the idea this thousand years stretches back to the first coming of Christ when there was no beast (in the sense of the book of Revelation) and there was no ruler to be cast into the lake of fire, as recorded in Revelation 19:20.

Buried in this passage, in the normal narrative and the description of the events which follow the second coming of Christ, is a clear indication it refers to a period after the second coming of Christ, not before. In the nature of the case—inasmuch as it declares these martyrs lived and reigned with Christ a thousand years—it is obvious that they died, Christ came, they were resurrected, and then they lived a thousand years. This makes clear that the millennial Kingdom is an event subsequent to the second coming of Christ. If so, it supports the idea that Christ will reign on earth for a thousand years.

To be explicit, the apostle says, "But the rest of the dead lived not again until the thousand years were finished" (v. 5). Referring to the resurrection of these martyrs, he states: "This is the first resurrection. Blessed and holy is he that has part in the first resurrection; on such the second death hath no power, but they shall be priests of God and of Christ, and shall reign with Him a thousand years" (Rev 20:6).

The passage puzzles some because they say, "How can this event be called the *first* resurrection? Has not the Church been resurrected? Has not Christ been resurrected? How can the resurrection of these martyred dead subsequent to Christ's second coming and the establishment of His Kingdom, be 'first'?"

It is obvious it is not first in the sense there was no preceding resurrection. The context prohibits this. What it says is this: the resurrection of the righteous comes first; the resurrection of the wicked comes next; and between the two events is at least a thousand years. This again is a passage for which the amillennialist interpretation has no reasonable interpretation. You simply cannot dismiss a thousand years with events that begin it and events which conclude it, and just wipe it off the books as if it does not exist. But how do we explain this first resurrection?

I take it that all the resurrections of the righteous are together called the resurrections which are first, in contrast to the resurrection of the wicked which is last. The first resurrection includes the resurrection of Jesus Christ; it includes the resurrection of the dead in Christ at the rapture of the Church; it includes the tribulation dead who are raised at the time Christ comes to set up His Kingdom; and it includes the resurrection of all the Old Testament saints, whether they are raised at the rapture or at the second coming. In either case they are all raised first.

At the begininng of the millennial Kingdom there are no righteous dead in the grave. All the righteous have been raised first. In the order of events these are first, and second comes a thousand-year reign on earth, and third comes the final resurrection recorded later in this chapter. It deals exclusively with those who have not trusted the Lord, whose names are not written in the Book of Life.

To the passage here about the Millennium we can add those of the Old Testament that describe Christ's glorious Kingdom on earth, where Israel will be a blessed nation and the Gentiles will bask in the righteous judgment of Christ; but we also have events which bring this reign to a close. "When the thousand years are expired, Satan shall be loosed out of his prison, and shall go out to deceive the nations which are in the four quarters of the earth, Gog and Magog [ruler and people], to gather them together to battle, the number of whom is as the sand of the sea" (Rev 20:7-8).

The Scriptures go on, "And they went up on the breadth of the earth and compassed the camp of the saints about and the beloved city, and fire came down from God out of heaven and devoured them" (Rev 20:9). This event comes at the close of the millennial Kingdom. When the thousand years have expired and the righteous government of Christ is continued for this period, then Satan is loosed again and immediately he deceives many who follow him; they attempt to surround Jerusalem and take the capital of the world by force. The Scriptures record that fire comes down from God out of heaven and destroys them.

Now the question has been raised, Where do these people come from who follow Satan? At the second coming of Christ all the wicked are put to death. That is made clear in the judgment of the nations, the parable of the wheat and the tares, the parable of the good and bad fish, and similar passages. All adults who worshiped the beast, the world ruler, and did not worship Christ, will be destroyed at the second coming of Christ.

Those who are on earth at the time of the second coming of Christ and who have put their trust in Him, whether Jew or Gentile, will move on into the millennial Kingdom. In contrast to those who have been translated or resurrected, they will still have natural bodies. The millennial prophecies of the Old Testament picture them reigning with Christ on earth and living normal lives, bearing children, planting crops, building houses, building cities—going through the normal functions of life, until a whole new generation of people are born during this thousand years. Because Christ reigns on earth, all must at least profess faith in Him. But then, as now, all who outwardly profess will not necessarily be believers.

When Satan is loosed, those who have superficially believed in Christ, who have never been born again and have gone through the outward motions without inner reality, will be subject to the temptation to rebel against Christ and to show their true colors. This is the origin of the company who follow Satan, deceived by him and led to oppose Jesus Christ and the saints.

Verse 10 states, "The devil that deceived them was cast into the lake of fire and brimstone." He had been bound for a thousand years; he had not been in torment. Now he is cast into the lake of fire, a place prepared for the devil and his angels. It tells us that he is cast into the lake of fire and brimstone where the beast and the false prophet are, and shall be tormented day and night forever.

It is significant that after a thousand years the beast and false prophet who were cast into the lake of fire are still there; they are still in existence. Human life does not end, but is destined for either heaven or hell. Here it is plain, in fact, if you translate it literally, the verb "shall be tormented" is in the plural, meaning that the devil and the beast and the false prophet shall be tormented day and night forever.

In the Scriptures which follow, the judgment of the great white throne comes in verses 11-15. Anyone not found written in the Book of Life is cast into the lake of fire and judged according to his works, a judgment that takes place at the *end* of the millennium, not the *beginning*. It logically follows the sequence of events in this chapter.

As one comes to Revelation 20, admittedly in a book where there is much symbolic presentation and John saw much by way of vision, it is clear it was God's intent that through a symbolic presentation literal prophetic truth should be communicated. The early chapters of the Revelation are a stirring presentation of events leading up to the second coming of Christ.

In chapter 19, the second coming of Christ itself is revealed. In chapter 20, the epilogue, the Kingdom which will follow, beginning with the resurrection of the righteous dead, those who were beheaded for the witness of Jesus in the Tribulation, is given. Satan was bound at the beginning of the Millennium, and he is loosed again at the end of the thousand years. Then rebellion breaks out and there is judgment. In the verses which follow, the final judgment of all the wicked dead is presented as the last in the series.

Chapters 21 and 22 reveal the new heaven and the new earth and describe the new Jerusalem, the home of the saints. Here the saints will live in the presence of the Lord forever.

Certainly these are stirring events, but the question of whether the world will see a thousand-year reign of Christ, and Christ will actually reign on earth for a thousand years, is not just a theological question. It is the question as to whether the Bible means what it says. The Bible is as articulate in detailing future events as it is in describing the great historic fact that Christ died for our sins and rose again.

The One who came once and literally fulfilled hundreds of prophecies related to His first coming, will come again and fulfill, equally literally, prophecies related to His second coming. We can be looking to that glad moment when there will be the shout from the blue and Christ will literally come for us to be with Him forever.

17

The Day of Resurrection

JOHN F. WALVOORD

ONE OF THE CENTRAL TRUTHS of our Christian faith is that man lives forever. In contrast to all other forms of organic life, that live and die and pass from the scene, man alone continues forever. And even if he dies, whether righteous or unrighteous, he is subject, in God's time, to resurrection. There is no end to human existence.

Because this is a central fact of our faith, it is understandable that some theologians have taught there will be one final event in the course of human life, in which all will be raised, all will be judged, and all will pass into eternal existence.

But the Scriptures, in presenting the details of resurrection, indicate instead of one great resurrection there will be a series of resurrections, ending with the resurrection of the wicked. This is brought out very clearly in the twentieth chapter of Revelation. It comes as the climax to the second coming of Christ, described so graphically in chapter 19.

Revelation 20:4 reveals those who have died as martyrs in the tragic time of trouble preceding Christ's coming to set up His Kingdom will live again. "They lived and reigned with Christ a thousand years" (Rev 20:4). Then it adds, "But the rest of the dead lived not again until the thousand years were finished. This [the resurrection of the righteous] is the first resurrection." Accordingly, the resurrection of the righteous occurs at least a thousand years before the resurrection of the wicked. So it is not true that all men are raised at the same time and sent to their eternal destiny in one grand event. It is rather a series of resurrections.

A further problem appears in this text when it refers to those raised at Christ's coming to set up His Kingdom, as a part of the first resurrection. The Bible doctrine of resurrection includes the revelation that there have been resurrections which have preceded the resurrection of the martyred dead at the end of the Great Tribulation before Christ's return to set up His Kingdom. The first resurrection was that of Christ Himself. In keeping with His prediction He said, "I have power to lay it down, and I have power to take it again" (Jn 10:18). That is what history has recorded. In 1 Corinthians 15, the central fact is the resurrection of Christ, the cornerstone upon which our Christian faith is built.

It gives us confidence Jesus Christ is what He claimed to be, the Son of God. Only God in human form could lay down His life by an act of His will, and raise His dead body from the grave by the act of His will. That is why, when the disciples and the godly women who followed Christ went out to the tomb on that first resurrection day, they found the stone rolled away. The tomb was empty, and in it lay eloquent testimony that Christ had risen from the grave. The graveclothes probably still conformed to the form of His human body.

Matthew 27:51-53 also records that at the resurrection of Christ there was a token resurrection; some of the tombs in Jerusalem had opened, and those in the tombs later appeared in the city as witnesses to Christ's resurrection. This resurrection is not explained anywhere else in the Word of God, but it seems to be a fulfillment of what was anticipated in faith in the offering of the firstfruits of harvest. In the instructions given to the Jews, they were to bring a handful of grain to the priest at the beginning of the harvest season. This was a token of the harvest yet ahead, and emphasized God as the Giver of the harvest. So in the doctrine of resurrection we have firstfruits, a token resurrection anticipating what was yet to be fulfilled, the resurrection of all the righteous dead.

The night before His crucifixion Christ told His disciples He was going to leave them, but He was going to heaven to prepare a place for them in the Father's house. In John 14:3 He declared, "If I go and prepare a place for you, I will come again, and receive you unto myself; that where I am, there ye may be also." While He did not explain it to the disciples, and they were not prepared to receive this glorious truth, He was declaring the wonderful fact that one day Christ would come for His entire Church.

It was given to the apostle Paul to expound this doctrine. In connection with the restatement of great fundamental truths of the faith to the Corinthian church, he brought out the great truth of Christ coming for His Church (1 Co 15:51-58). The chapter reveals the historic fact that Christ died for our sins, according to the Scripture, that He was buried, that He rose again the third day, according to the Scripture, and that His resurrection was attested by many witnesses, including 500 at once. The apostle Paul argued that on the basis of the fact of the resurrection of Christ, believers can rest secure in the fact that if we die, we will be raised.

God's order is that all human beings of all kinds and classifications and cultures and colors will be raised from the dead in God's time. Our present bodies are not suited for eternity. Believers need a heavenly body, a spiritual body, a new body, as Paul brings out specifically in this chapter.

Paul then introduces a truth not found in the Old Testament, and clearly not recorded in any of the teachings of Christ, which he had announced earlier to the Thessalonians and in his preaching—that is, when the Lord comes it will be the day of resurrection for Christians who have died, but living Christians will go to heaven without dying.

Paul declares this glorious truth, "Behold, I show you a mystery; we shall not all sleep, but we shall all be changed, in a moment, in a twinkling of an eye at the last trump: for the trumpet shall sound, and the dead shall be raised incorruptible, and we shall be changed. For this corruptible must put on incorruption, and this mortal must put on immortality" (1 Co 15:51-53).

As Paul brings out here and elsewhere in Scripture, our present bodies are not suited for heaven. First of all, our present bodies are sinful bodies, the kind of body we inherited from our parents. Men do not have to be taught to do wrong; it is a very natural thing for the human race to do wrong. As Isaiah the prophet said, "All we like sheep have gone astray; we have turned every one to his own way" (Is 53:6). This is the normal course of human nature.

Paul wrote the Ephesians that they were dead in trespasses and sins (Eph 2:1). This is our natural estate. Even when we come to Christ and experience the amazing miracle of the new birth and become new creatures in Christ and our bodies become the temple of God, it is still true our bodies of earth are bodies capable of sinning, bodies not suited for heaven.

In God's provision for us in our salvation in Christ, God promised that when we die and are resurrected, or translated, at the coming of the Lord, we will receive a body that will never sin again, one gloriously suited to serving the Lord perfectly throughout all eternity. This is a marvelous token of the power of the death of Christ, the power of His resurrection, and the power of the grace of God. In eternity believers will be living illustrations (Eph 2) of what the grace of God can accomplish in taking a person who once was dead in sin and making him alive in Christ.

The Scriptures point out two other things wrong with our bodies. One, our bodies are corruptible. Our bodies are subject to age. We grow older, and in due time the bouncing baby so full of energy becomes the old man who just creeps along. All it takes is time. This is not a suitable body for heaven.

In the resurrection and the translation of the Church our bodies are suddenly going to be vibrant with life. We have never known perfect health in this life. We have always had in us the principles of death, decay, and disease; but when the Lord comes and the day of resurrection takes place, both those raised from the dead and those translated will receive new bodies vibrantly alive and capable of serving the Lord. What a glorious prospect for all who have infirmity in the flesh. And what a release it will be from the bondage of this body of death, as Paul calls it (Ro 7:24), a body not suited for eternity, that needs to be replaced by a new body.

As the apostle points out, our present bodies are also mortal. While our souls continue forever, our bodies are subject to death. It really is amazing, when you consider all the things which occur in the human body that could cause instant death, that our bodies continue as long as they do. Within us a marvelous process of restoration keeps us going for many years. But we are subject to death. And whether by accident or something that suddenly goes wrong, or through some creeping disease that gradually robs us of strength, these bodies are subject to death.

A body subject to death is not suitable for the presence of the Lord forever. So we have the wonderful prospect of being in the presence of the Lord forever in a body without sin, sickness, pain, or decay, a body perpetually young and vibrant with life and one that will never know death. Our body will be God's handiwork, God's perfect creation, a demonstration of the marvelous grace of God that comes to us as we put our faith in Jesus Christ.

The Scriptures do not tell us when this event will take place. Every passage on this event simply tells us to look for His coming. There are tremendous prophetic events which follow the coming of Christ for His Church, such as God's great movement among the nations in the end time, God's dealing with apostate Christendom, and God's working in His people Israel. In our contemporary life is eloquent witness we may be living in the very last days of the Church on earth, the days preceding Christ's coming to receive His own. We live in an age of prophetic fulfillment, so everything we do is colored by the fact the Lord may be coming very soon. I believe this is what God intended.

In the earlier revelation the apostle Paul gave to the Thessalonians he discussed the matter of the imminency of the Lord's return and of the order of events relating to it. The Thessalonians were a group of young Christians. Paul had gone to Thessalonica in Macedonia and had preached, according to Acts 17, for three weeks, and a multitude were saved.

But the amazing work of God in leading so many to Christ stirred up opposition. The result was that Paul was in danger of losing his life as a martyr. This was not God's plan for Paul at this time. He still had much to do for God before he would finally lay down his life as a martyr. So, accompanied by Silas and Timothy, he left Thessalonica.

When he left, he left part of his heart behind. These young believers, scarcely a month old in the faith, were without a Bible, a pastor, an organized church, or a place to turn for further light and help in their Christian faith. So the apostle sent Timothy back to see how they were getting along. Because he was less conspicuous than Paul as a leader, he was able to slip into town, have a few days of fellowship with these young believers, and then return to Paul to report how gloriously God had undertaken for this young church.

Their witness was so effective that everyone in the town was talking about this Jesus who had died and risen again. The talk up and down the trade route which went through Thessalonica was about this new faith, so different from any other faith they had ever heard of—a faith based upon a Man who was God and who had died and risen again from the grave, a Man who could forgive sin, a Man who could give eternal life.

But the Thessalonians were also under great persecution. Some of their number had died. We do not know whether they were martyrs or whether they died of natural causes, but their death so soon after their newborn faith in Christ, was a matter of deep concern to the Thessalonian church; and it raised theological questions in their minds. Apparently, in those few days Paul had been with them he had taught them not only the truth of the death and resurrection of Christ, but also the wonderful truth of resurrection and Christ's coming for His living Church. While they did not understand it all, they were looking for the coming of the Lord.

But this very fact raised questions. What about these Christians who had died? When would they be raised from the dead? Would they be raised at the time Christ came for His living Church, or would they have to wait until after the time of predicted trouble at the consummation of things when Christ would come back to set up His Kingdom? So they sent back by Timothy questions which apparently he could not answer.

In reply to these inquiries the apostle wrote the section in 1 Thessalonians 4:13-18. Paul declared unto them, "I would not have you to be ignorant, brethren, concerning them who are asleep, that ye sorrow not, even as others which have no hope." He did not want them to be ignorant Christians who did not know the wonderful hope that we have in Christ. He did not want them to sorrow in the loss of their loved ones as those who did not expect to see them again. We Christians have a wonderful hope, and God wants us to understand it; He wants us to enjoy it; He wants us to be comforted by it.

Paul goes on in verse 14, "For if we believe that Jesus died and rose again, even so them also who sleep in Jesus will God bring with him." In other words, just as certain as the historic fact that Christ died and rose, so also equally certain is the prophetic fact that Christ is coming again, and when He comes He will bring those who are asleep in Jesus with Him.

What happens when a Christian dies today? We have a funeral service, and we reverently lay their bodies to rest; but they are not in the tomb. We believe to be absent from the body is to be present with the Lord (2 Co 5:8), and we rejoice and are comforted by the fact that our loved ones, who in their last days may have suffered much, are now free from all the cares and ills of this life, radiant with joy in the presence of the Saviour.

When Christ comes in this event He will bring these souls from heaven back with Him to the earthly sphere. Why is He going to do this? As the Scriptures which follow tell us, their bodies will be resurrected and their souls will enter their resurrected bodies to be united forever.

Paul goes on:

> For this we say unto you by the word of the Lord, [by direct revelation] that we who are alive and remain unto the coming of the Lord shall not prevent [precede] them who are asleep. For the Lord himself shall descend from heaven with a shout, with the voice of the archangel and with the trump of God: and the dead in Christ shall rise first: then we who are alive and remain shall be caught up together with them in the clouds to meet the Lord in the air, and so shall we ever be with the Lord (1 Th 4:15-17).

In these reassuring words to the Thessalonians Paul first answers their question on when the dead will be raised in relationship to living Christians who are translated. They are going to be raised just a moment before. They are going to be raised first. There will be no waiting time. While the Bible does not explain it, the most simple explanation is probably the best. We lay their bodies in the grave, below the level of earth's activities. They have a little farther to go, and so they are raised first. Then they join us as we are caught up to meet the Lord in the air.

What a dramatic event it will be! Suppose it happened to-day. As far as Scriptural revelation is concerned, it could, for this is a dateless event; and because so many things occur in the world that seem to be a preparation for fulfillment of prophecies scheduled after the rapture of the Church, it makes us realize Christ's coming for His own, the rapture, could occur any day. Suppose it happened. What would occur?

First of all, the Lord would descend from heaven where He is at the right hand of the Father, interceding for us. He would descend to the air above the earth. He would issue a shout, which is a command, accompanied by the voice of the archangel. This refers to Michael, the head of all the holy angels, who has been engaged in ceaseless warfare against Satan and the powers of wickedness. His voice is heard. Then, there is the trump of God, which Paul refers to in 1 Corinthians 15:52 as the last trump. It is the final call for the Church.

The Church has heard the call of the Gospel and responded by faith in Christ. The Church has heard the call to service and dedication, and has responded by giving their lives to Christ. But now this is the final call, the last trump. When it sounds the dead in Christ are going to hear; they will be raised from the dead. Then we who are alive and remain shall be caught up together with them in the clouds to meet the Lord in the air, and so shall we ever be with the Lord.

From other Scriptures we gather we are going to go from our meeting place, a rendezvous in the blue, in procession to the Father's house, to heaven itself, there to be welcomed by the holy angels. In the presence of the Lord we will rejoice in what God has done in completing His Church, His body, His bride, the body of believers, Jew and Gentile, who through the ages have found life in Jesus Christ. So shall we ever be with the Lord. As the song, "Ten Thousand Times Ten Thousand," states it, what an amazing meeting this will be, families reunited, loved ones separated by distance and death now regathered; and then, most glorious of all, we will see our Saviour face to face.

Of all the things we will talk about in eternity, one of the recurring subjects will be the thrill when, for the first time, we see the Saviour, whom having not seen we have loved. When we see Him in all His glory, He will completely capture our affection, our obedience, our worship, our loyalty, and eternally we will have no greater joy than to live for Him and express how much we love Him and how much we appreciate the wonderful salvation that we have in Him.

In 1 Thessalonians 4 Paul concludes the passage, "Wherefore, comfort one another with these words." In our hour of sorrow and grief, as we lay our Christian loved ones away temporarily from our sight, how wonderful it is to know it is only for time and not for eternity, that we will meet again, perhaps very soon, if the Lord comes. Actually, the word translated "comfort" is inadequate to explain the full meaning of the New Testament Greek. The word means to encourage, to urge on, to excite. We are to be excited about the wonderful prospect before us, which should help us be faithful.

In 1 Corinthians 15 the apostle, after recounting our victory when death is swallowed up in victory, concludes this will be a great victory through Christ: "Therefore, my beloved brethren, be ye stedfast, unmoveable, always abounding in the work of the Lord, forasmuch as ye know that your labour is not in vain in the Lord" (v. 58).

It is possible to become so enamored of prophecy, the study of the fulfillment of prophecy, and the details coming out in the prophetic program, that prophecy could become an end in itself. Some are very curious about future events, and never tire of looking up some new facet of the prophetic Word. I believe there is a proper place for thorough biblical study of prophecy. But as presented in the Bible, prophecy is not intended simply to satisfy our curiosity, nor to enlarge our understanding of biblical doctrine, or our capacity to explain strange texts in Scripture. Prophecy is given to us for very practical reasons.

As one studies the entire prophetic Word, whether in the Old or the New Testament, he finds prophecy is always followed by practical exhortation. It may be a call to a group in apostasy to come back to the Lord, or warning of judgment, or it may be words of encouragement. But in every case the truth of God's prophetic program is intended to spur us on, to make us faithful and steadfast. The word "stedfast" means to sit down, it means to put your weight on, to rest on. But it does not infer we should be immovable in our Christian faith. Some people are always taking a stand for something. There are times we need to stand, but we also need to move.

Here we are told that we should be unmovable, because we are resting upon the rock, Christ Jesus; but we are not to be immobile. Rather we should be "always abounding in the work of the Lord, forasmuch as ye know that your labor is not in vain in the Lord." Why? Because when the Lord comes and we are caught up into His presence, we will be judged at the judgment seat of Christ. It will be a time of victory, a time of reward, and a time when God is going to recognize those who have been faithful to Him.

As we face the challenge of life, and the fact that Christ could come at any moment, we should ask ourselves, "Are we ready for His coming?" Obviously, this one resurrection is singled out from a whole series, such as that of the Tribulation saints and the Old Testament saints. Later on there is the resurrection of the wicked at the end of the Millennium. Our resurrection is only one in a series. The wonderful fact is it could be very soon; in the light of this, we should be ready.

How can we be ready? First, by making certain of our personal faith in Jesus Christ. We are not made ready for the rapture by joining a church, however good the church may be, or by being religious, no matter how religious we may be. It requires a supernatural work of God. Christ has promised, and the Word has promised, that when we believe on the Lord Jesus Christ, we are saved. This is the first and basic preparation.

Christ said, "No man cometh unto the Father but by me." It is a personal matter; it is not something the church can do, or religion can do, or money can do, or even good works can do. It is by grace because God loves us, because Christ died for us. Then, if we put our faith in Christ, He is indeed our Lord and Saviour.

What else can we do but present our bodies as a living sacrifice, and live every day for Him until Jesus comes in glad expectation? It could be today we will see Him face to face!

18

The Eternal Kingship of Christ

CHARLES LEE FEINBERG

OF ALL THE THEMES of prophetic Scripture none appeals more strongly to the believer than that which relates to the Lord Jesus Christ. He is the theme of all prophecy (cf. Rev 19:10). What makes for great preaching, great theology, and great exposition is the exaltation of the person and work of Christ. From a number of passages on the eternal kingship of Christ, we choose John to strike the keynote:

> Then Pilate entered into the judgment hall again, and called Jesus, and said unto him, Art thou the King of the Jews? Jesus answered him, Sayest thou this thing of thyself, or did others tell it thee of me? Pilate answered, Am I a Jew? Thine own nation and the chief priests have delivered thee unto me. What hast thou done? Jesus answered, My kingdom is not of this world; if my kingdom were of this world, then would my servants fight, that I should not be delivered to the Jews; but now is my kingdom not from [here]. Pilate therefore said unto him, Art thou a king then? Jesus answered, Thou sayest that I am a king. To this end was I born, and for this cause came I into the world, that I should bear witness unto the truth. Every one that is of the truth heareth my voice (Jn 18:33-37).

A few preliminary remarks are in order. The paramount theme under discussion and in dispute was the actuality of the kingship of Jesus of Nazareth. Pilate's questions are slanted in that direction. The words *king* and *kingdom* appear in this portion six times. Furthermore, verse 36 cannot be taken to mean Christ never intended to have a kingdom on earth, for the verse only states His method in setting it up is not after the manner of men, who resort to conflict to sustain their temporal kingdoms. Earthly dominions are commenced, carried on, and concluded with strife and carnage. Finally, it is a misunderstanding of the Greek idiom to interpret Christ's answer (v. 37) as inferring that what Pilate asked was one thing, and Christ evaded the issue by stating that what Pilate said need not be the case. Christ's reply was strongly in the affirmative, as the next clauses show, when He declared it was for kingship He was born into the world.

It is a sad commentary on the manner in which the Word of God has been handled. The teaching of the Bible on the kingly office of Christ has been grossly neglected on one hand, or shamefully distorted on the other. There is much Scripture for the prophetic ministry of our Lord. Deuteronomy 18:15-18 predicted that, because Israel at Sinai requested a mediator, the Lord acquiesced by indicating the establishment of the order of the prophets to be climaxed in the prophetic office of the Messiah, the ultimate Prophet.

Isaiah 50:4-7 foretold the Servant of the Lord would have the hearing ear to get the message from the Lord aright and the instructed tongue to speak it forth truthfully and effectively. These are two essentials of prophetic service. It would not be difficult to carry this truth through the New Testament, as in John 4 where the woman of Samaria recognized in Jesus the Prophet prophesied in the Pentateuch.

Similarly, there is good basis in Scripture for the priestly ministry of the coming Messiah. Who can fail to see the direction of the Levitical sacrifices and the priesthood? One reading of the epistle to the Hebrews will settle the issue. All pointed unmistakably to the priestly work of the Lord Jesus. And how could one misread Isaiah 52:13—53:12, with its indisputable delineation of Messiah as the Priest in His sacrifice (esp. vv. 4-6)? He is the sacrifice and the officiating Priest as well.

Similarly, there is a vast body of truth on His eternal kingship. Because the devil is a consummate counterfeiter from the beginning, he instituted a kingdom on earth as early as Genesis 10:10, the first mention of a kingdom in the Bible. It was the kingdom of the rebel Nimrod (so the meaning of his name). Then from Genesis to the Revelation there is a line of truth concerning misgovernment, misleading, and misrule from Nimrod to the beast of the Revelation. On the other hand, from Genesis to Revelation God has made clear whom He has in mind for true leadership, godly rule, and valid sovereignty.

The great prophetic theme of the eternal kingship of Christ lends itself to a simple fourfold division, embracing all the testimony of the Bible. The first is:

THE KINGSHIP PROMISED

The first reference to God's King is found in Genesis in the prophecy of Jacob. Foretelling concerning Judah he said:

> Judah, thou art he whom thy brethren shall praise: thy hand shall be in the neck of thine enemies; thy father's children shall bow down before thee. Judah is a lion's whelp: from the prey, my son, thou art gone up: he stooped down, he crouched as a lion, and as an old lion. Who shall rouse him up? The scepter shall not depart from Judah, nor a lawgiver from between his feet, until Shiloh come; and unto him shall the gathering of the people be. Binding his foal unto the vine, and his ass's colt unto the choice vine, he washed his garments in wine, and his clothes in the blood of grapes. His eyes shall be red with wine, and his teeth white with milk (49:8-12).

The portion speaks of prevailing in conflict, a powerful rule, a peaceful realm, a prosperous commonwealth, and personal beauty, all centering in the King from Judah. This Scripture links eternal kingship with the tribe of Judah.

But as years blended into centuries, the tribe of Judah grew and expanded. Which one of the many families in the tribe of Judah was to be the honored one to cradle the coming King? The answer is found in 2 Samuel 7:10-17, known as the Davidic covenant. Without an understanding of this covenant the student of the Bible will make a shambles of the Gospel of Matthew and all the passages on the eternal kingship of Messiah. When David longed to build God a material house, a temple, it was not permitted because of his many campaigns in a lifetime of victories.

But God is no man's debtor. The Lord promised David a royal house, a dynasty, an eternal rule among his descendants. Psalm 89 reveals the steadfastness of the covenant in spite of David's compounded sin. Why? Because the Davidic covenant is an unconditional one, where the ultimate fulfillment is guaranteed by the reliability of the Lord and not man. As time passed the prophets enlarged on the theme of the king in David's line. You need only compare Isaiah 7:14; 9:6-7; Jeremiah 23:5-6; Ezekiel 37:22-25; Daniel 7:13-14; and Micah 5:2 among others. Actually, the Old Testament is a finger pointing to the coming King.

Is it any wonder, then, that orthodox Jews await to this hour the coming of Messiah? In the daily recital of their creed (coming down from the medieval philosopher and rabbi, Maimonides) they declare: "I believe with complete faith in the coming of the Messiah; and even though he tarry, I will wait for him every coming day." Thus over all the Old Testament there may be written the kingship promised.

The second division of the subject is:

THE KINGSHIP PRESENTED

God gave ample promises on Messiah's kingship in the Old Testament. When we turn to the four gospels, we find God did not permit those promises to go unfulfilled. In the fulness of time the King came to earth.

The first verse of the first book in our New Testament canon strangely places the name of David before Abraham, when there was a period of about a millennium between them. Why? Because the Spirit of God will allow no reader to get beyond the first verse without declaring that He has not forgotten the covenant of God to David regarding a king. Yet, why is the genealogy constructed purposely around fourteen generations in three groupings? Why just fourteen? The numerical value of the consonants (there are no vowels in the Hebrew alphabet) in the name of David comes to exactly fourteen ($D = 4$, $V = 6$, $D = 4$).

Again, the Spirit of God alerts all with emphasis on the importance of the Davidic covenant. He came to His land, His throne, and His kingdom (Jn 1:11). He presented Himself as King and offered a kingdom. See Matthew 3:2; 4:17; 10:7; and study them carefully. But a king must have laws for the orderly government of his realm. So King Messiah enunciates the laws of His Kingdom in Matthew 5-7. He offered Himself as King (Mt 21:1-5) and was rejected in His kingly offer (Jn 18:37; 19:14-15). The accusation over His head on the cross bore His claim and His presentation of Himself as King. Nor would God allow this claim to be muted (Jn 19:19, 21). It must stand in all its force, because it was every whit valid. The offer of the Kingdom and the rejection of the King are brought out in Matthew 22:1-7. Undeniably, Jesus Christ came as the promised King and offered the predicted Kingdom.

On May 17, 1927 the Associated Press from Madrid carried an item of news on King Alfonso III. He had celebrated his twenty-fifth anniversary as king of Spain. It was also his forty-first birthday. He was born on May 17, 1886, five months after the death of his father. He had been a king longer than any other living ruler. He was born a king, although he was not crowned until his eighteenth birthday. Men may claim to be born kings, and in their limited sense it is true; but how much more true of the Lord Jesus, God's King?

The third division of the theme is:

THE KINGSHIP POSTPONED

When the King was rejected in His rightful claims, we must remember the fault was not with the promise of the Kingdom, nor with the Promisor of the Kingdom (God the Father), nor with the promised King (Christ). This being true, does it seem consistent with the method of Scripture that God would allow His promise of kingship to be nullified or go unfulfilled? The Scriptures answer in the negative. From Acts through Jude, the Kingdom is seen as postponed in its full earthly manifestation. It is true that from God's viewpoint nothing was postponed. But it certainly was from Israel's standpoint.

A clear parallel is the period of Israel's wandering in the wilderness after the rebellion at Kadesh-barnea. As far as God was concerned, nothing took Him by surprise. But there was a postponement of entrance into the land of promise for Israel until the rebellious generation had died out. It is correct and defensible to hold that the Kingdom was postponed, just as surely as it was previously offered. Note a number of texts. Let us choose Luke 19:11-12:

> And as they heard these things, he added, and spoke a parable, because he was near to Jerusalem, and because they thought that the kingdom of God should immediately appear [mark this carefully]. He said, therefore, A certain nobleman went into a far country to receive for himself a kingdom, and to return.

The passage speaks of a definite break in time as the nobleman goes into a far country to be invested with a kingdom. The Kingdom was not to be set up (else how explain the mystery parables of Matthew 13) because of the rejection and absence of the King from His realm, and therefore would be in abeyance until His return.

Those who oppose this position tell us this view is impossible because, if Israel had accepted Christ, the cross would have been bypassed. This is shallow reasoning. Was it a bona fide test when God commanded Adam and Eve not to eat of the forbidden tree? Then how was it God already had prepared a Lamb from eternity for the sin of Adam and the human race? One does not nullify the other. Besides, Daniel 9:26 places in direct juxtaposition the cross and the matter of the Kingdom. Messiah is to be cut off (the cross clearly) and have nothing (the Kingdom).

What was it He had nothing of while here? Not disciples, not followers, not divine approval, not power to work miraculous deeds and preach marvelous truths. There was one thing He had nothing of—the predicted Kingdom. Furthermore, if Israel had accepted Christ, then Isaiah 53 and other passages would have proved false. Scripture does not contradict itself, though it may be difficult for us to reconcile certain portions.

Moreover, other Scriptures confirm the validity of the postponement of the kingdom. Compare the promise of rule on David's throne (Lk 1:32, 33) with His position now (Rev 3:21) and the prospect of Matthew 25:31. To Hebrews who were expecting a king on David's throne, yet had rejected him in the Person of Jesus of Nazareth, the sacred writer of the Epistle to the Hebrews emphasized the session of Christ at God's right hand (1:3; 8:1; 10:12; 12:20). With every mention the writer points out Christ as seated elsewhere than on His earthly Davidic throne.

J. H. Jowett once said when the emperor of Germany dismissed his great counselor Bismarck, *Punch* in London had a cartoon by Tenniel representing a great liner. Bismarck was just leaving the vessel, while the emperor watched the departing guide with haughty self-satisfaction. The cartoon was entitled "Dropping the Pilot." Said Jowett, that cartoon represented experiences in his own life. But instead of a human, fallible statesman, he had dismissed the infallible God. He had dropped the eternal Pilot. He had called it self-dependence, and with a great show of courtesy he had bowed his Lord out of the boat. Then he had taken the helm into his own hands, and steered by his own counsels. The end, understandably, was agony, sorrow, and loss. So it was with Israel when they rejected the King; they dropped the Eternal King, and the Kingdom was postponed.

But there is a final and fourth division which tells us of:

THE KINGSHIP PERFECTED

The book of Revelation contains the consummation of all things, including the finale of the kingship as well. Despite all views to the contrary, Christ will yet be the eternal King in manifestation and realization (Ps 110). All the promises of the kingdom and kingship will be perfected and performed for evermore. The Scriptures are both clear and full of this phase of the truth under consideration. Refresh your memory on what Psalms 2, 24, 45, 72, and 110 relate concerning the coming Kingdom of the Redeemer of Israel. Notice again the eloquence of the prophets as the Spirit of God guides their minds and pens in Isaiah 32:1-2; Jeremiah 23:5-6 and 33:14-21; Ezekiel 34:23-24; Daniel 2:44-45; 7:13-14; and Zechariah 9:9-11. Observe also the heights of truth opened by Paul in 1 Corinthians 15:24-28 and Philippians 2:5-11, and concluded by John in Revelation 19:16.

One of Queen Victoria's chaplains, in preaching before her at Windsor, made the coming glory and reign of Christ the subject of his message. After the service the queen, who was always a most attentive listener, spoke to him on the topic he had chosen and said, "Oh, how I wish the Lord might come during my lifetime."

"Why," asked the preacher, "does your majesty feel this very earnest desire?"

The queen answered, with lips quivering, "I should so love to lay my crown at His feet."

In a coming day all kings and queens will do so, willingly or unwillingly.

There is but one rightful, eternal King, the Lord Jesus Christ. God is committed to the program of setting Him on His rightful throne. He who had the agony will have the acclaim, for the blood the blessing, for the cross the crown, for the death the delight, for the gore the glory, for the judgment the joy, for the misery the majesty, for the ridicule the reign, for the suffering the satisfaction, for the thorns the throne, and for the wounds the welcome of billions of souls!

Have you noticed how rich the hymnology of the Church is on this exalted theme? Hear it.

> Crown Him with many crowns,
> The Lamb upon His throne;
> Hark! how the heavenly anthem drowns
> All music but its own!
> Awake, my soul, and sing,
> Of Him who died for thee,
> And hail Him as thy matchless King,
> Through all eternity.
>
> M. BRIDGES

> Jesus shall reign where'er the sun
> Does his successive journeys run;
> His kingdom spread from shore to shore,
> Till moons shall wax and wane no more.
>
> ISAAC WATTS

> All hail the power of Jesus' name!
> Let angels prostrate fall;
> Bring forth the royal diadem,
> And crown Him Lord of all.
>
> E. PERRONET

Even so, come Lord Jesus!